Edmund J. (Edmund Janes) Carpenter

A Woman of Shawmut

A Romance of Colonial Times

Edmund J. (Edmund Janes) Carpenter

A Woman of Shawmut
A Romance of Colonial Times

ISBN/EAN: 9783744665407

Printed in Europe, USA, Canada, Australia, Japan

Cover: Foto ©Thomas Meinert / pixelio.de

More available books at **www.hansebooks.com**

A

WOMAN OF SHAWMUT

A Romance of Colonial Times

BY

EDMUND JANES CARPENTER

WITH ILLUSTRATIONS

By FRANK T. MERRILL

BOSTON

LITTLE, BROWN, AND COMPANY

1891

UNIVERSITY PRESS:
JOHN WILSON AND SON, CAMBRIDGE.

WILLIAM DEAN HOWELLS.

DEAR MR. HOWELLS, — I think I can never forget that delightful September day when I sat, with you, in your charming summer home at Nahant, and unfolded the plan of the simple story contained in these pages. To your kind encouragement and suggestions then given is due, in large degree, whatever measure of literary success may be claimed for this work. In gratitude for this kindness, therefore, as well as in admiration for your own qualities as a man of letters, I beg leave to inscribe to you this book; and remain

Yours, with regard and esteem,

E. J. CARPENTER.

THISTLE COTTAGE, MILTON,
August, 1891.

LIST OF ILLUSTRATIONS.

THE triple peaks of Shawmut rose clear and sharp against the cold, blue sky, and upon their summits rested the morning sunlight. The few warm days of early spring had long ago dissolved the last remnant of snow. In the forest of Rocksbury alone, hidden in the glades, lay little patches of white, through which a stray green shoot here and there sought to push itself. But the spring sunshine had beaten back into the forest depths the chill of winter, leaving a broad belt of warm woodland, where the fallen leaves rustled again as when, months before, they covered the earth. Now they were blown about in little heaps, eddying about the stumps and fallen logs, and filling the hollows. On the tree-tops the chipmunk chattered, and below him the robin chirped a welcome to the springtime. This was their domain. Save when the light tread of the Indian was heard in the forest, their sway was seldom disputed.

The broad surface of the basin of the Charles sparkled in the morning sunlight, and its ripples reflected the rays of gold and crimson which quivered on the hilltops and glanced downward. Little clouds of white, tinged with the sunrise glow, sailed slowly across the sky. A soft breeze, cajoling all Nature into song, just ruffled the surface of the bay. It was one of those warm, generous days of early spring which come once in a while at that season in New England, as if to console us for our long waiting, and to promise fuller joys in the days to come.

The chipmunk and the robin, on this May morning of 1640, failed to hold their undisputed sway in the forest of Rōcksbury. A step was heard among the rustling leaves, and the chipmunk shook his tail and flashed from tree to tree in sudden alarm. The robin turned his head, and ceased to plume his crimson breast as he looked downward upon the intruder. He saw a young man, attired in fantastic garb. A hat pointed in crown and generous of brim covered his head ; upon his shoulders hung long, curling locks of fair hair, which across the forehead was combed smoothly down and clipped squarely, much after the fashion followed by some young girls to-day; he wore a belted tunic, with broad buckle and ample skirt ; small-clothes confined at the knee with sad-colored ribbons, and heavy, knitted stockings covered his legs ; a broad, square linen collar lay upon his shoulders and breast ; and shoes with great rosettes of ribbon completed the costume.

Ezekiel Bolt had come forth from the quaint settlement of Shawmut, then a little hamlet engirdled by the sea. Before the day

broke he had risen, stolen softly through the
quiet streets of the village, traversed the
narrow "Neck," where two seas well-nigh
met, and skirted the shore of the bay. He
walked slowly along the sandy beach, his feet
crunching the moist pebbles. As he reached
the margin of the wood, the first ray of sunlight shot across the sky and lighted up the
beacon upon the distant hill with a glow, as
if the warning signal had suddenly burst into
flame. Ezekiel paused in his walk, and bared
his head to the morning breeze, as he gazed
out upon the placid water. A moment he
stood as if in worship, and then forth upon
the morning air burst from his lips the words
of the Puritan version of David's psalm : —

> "Fret not thyselfe because of those
>   That evill workers bee,
> Nor envious bee against the men
>   That work iniquity,
> For like unto the grasse they shall
>   Be cut down suddenly,
> And like unto the tender herb
>   They withering shall dye.

Upon the Lord put thou thy trust,
And be thou doing good,
So shalt thou dwell within the land,
And sure thou shalt have food.
See that thou set thy heart's delight
Also upon the Lord,
And the desyers of thy heart
To thee He will afford."[1]

The psalm ceased; and as the last echo died away over the hills, Ezekiel plunged into the forest. With eyes fixed upon the ground, he wandered up and down, pushing the dry leaves aside, and now and then stooping, as his search appeared to be rewarded. So quiet and gentle was he, that the startled robin resumed his song, and the squirrel, peeping from his door in a hollow tree, ceased to marvel at the invasion of private grounds.

An hour passed, two hours, and the sun climbed steadily into the heavens. The spring air lost its morning chill; the waves lost their

[1] For certain historical data and explanations, the reader is referred to the Appendix at the close of the book.

lines of crimson, and took on a deeper hue
of blue. Suddenly from out the Cambridge
shore shot a birch canoe. It had but a single
occupant, a young girl, who plied the paddle
with such energy and skill that she soon became distinctly seen. She, too, was clad in
the Puritan garb. A closely fitting cap covered the head; a broad white kerchief was
crossed upon the bosom, almost concealing
the gown of sombre hue; long gloves, which
covered the hands and arms, fell slightly away
from the short, simple sleeve, revealing a bit
of the arm as blooming as the soft cheeks.

With sturdy movements of the paddle the
light craft was propelled over the water toward
the Rocksbury shore. Then the girl ceased
to labor for a moment, and looked upward
and around. She gazed on the triple hills,
up whose sides were creeping the modest
homes of the people of Shawmut. She gazed
upon the blue sky above, and upon the broad
surface of the water; and then she, too, with

the spirit of devotion which characterized
those early settlers of Massachusetts Bay, gave
voice in song to the emotions with which her
nature throbbed in the freshness of the morning. Clear and sweet across the water came
the words of the psalm of trust : —

> "God is our refuge, strength, and help,
>   In troubles very neere,
> Therefore we will not be afrayd
>   Though th' earth removèd were.
> Though mountains move to midst of seas,
>   Though waters roaring make,
> And troubled be at whose swellings
>   Although the mountains shake."

Ezekiel paused as the words of the psalm
came wafted to the forest, and peering through
a glade discovered the canoe. A flush and
look of pleasure rose upon his face. Still he
appeared in doubt, and remained in his place
of concealment, watching intently the girl's
approach. The canoe, following two or three
vigorous strokes of the paddle, grounded lightly

upon the beach. The girl sprang out, and with a dexterous pull dragged the canoe high upon the shore. She ran lightly across the beach, climbed the grassy bank, and entered the forest. Again the squirrel and the robin fled in alarm. The young man, from his hiding-place, watched the maiden as she wandered slowly up and down, as he had done. Snatches of the psalm came bubbling from her lips at times. At others a slight frown gathered over her face, as if her search were not so successful as she had hoped. Now and then she stooped close to the ground, as had Ezekiel, and arose with a smile.

Occasionally Ezekiel would take a step forward, as if determined to advance at all hazards. Then he would check himself, and remain content with longing looks. At last the girl approached the spot where he stood, and glancing upward, saw him half concealed by a sturdy oak. With a little cry she turned to flee.

"Pray thee, good Mistress Penelope, do not fear. It is I."

"Ezekiel, is it thou?" said the girl. "What doest thou in the forest so early?"

"Nay, what doest thou, Penelope? I saw thee as thou crossed in thy canoe, and heard thy psalm. It is early for thee to go abroad, and so far from home. Dost thou not fear?"

"There is naught to fear. The Indian is my friend. Did I not bind up the wounds of the brave Wachita, as he lay in the forest, wounded by the deer? Did he not give me his canoe, and swear the fealty of his tribe to me? Have I aught to fear in the forest?"

"Thou art brave and true, Penelope. But tell me, what seekest thou in the forest?"

"I came, Ezekiel, hoping mayhap to find some of the early mayflowers, which blossom here. But they seem shy as yet."

"Hast found none, then?"

"Only these," said the maiden, as she laid her finger upon a small spray of the delicate

2

pink blossoms, which peeped forth from the folds of her kerchief.

"I sorrow for thy disappointment. But mayhap the blame may be with me."

"With thee, Ezekiel?"

"Yea, with me, Penelope."

"Thou speakest in riddles," said the girl.

"Nay, not so, for here behold the proof," said Ezekiel, as he drew forth from the ample crown of his hat, which he had held carefully before him, a large bunch of the fresh arbutus. The dew still sparkled on the delicate petals. The girl dropped her eyes in embarrassment, and with one foot pushed away the dry leaves, and softly tapped the ground.

"Wilt thou not take them, Penelope?" asked Ezekiel. "I plucked them for thee."

"For me, Ezekiel?" — and the blue eyes glanced up wonderingly.

"For thee alone, Penelope. Wilt thou not take them?"

"In truth, Ezekiel, and I would like them," answered Penelope:

Ezekiel stepped quickly to the girl's side, and placed the blossoms in her hand. Their eyes and their fingers met, and with the glance and the touch the blossoms fell upon the ground. Both blushed, then laughed. Ezekiel dropped upon one knee and, casting his hat upon the ground, gathered the scattered blossoms. Then, still kneeling, he again offered them to the blushing girl.

"But stay," said he, hesitating, "mayhap thou wilt drop them again."

"Indeed, good Master Ezekiel, it was thou, not I, who dropped them," said Penelope, with a little show of indignation and a deeper blush.

"Was it I, fair mistress? Mayhap it was. Stay yet again, and let me bind them for thee;" and Ezekiel quickly plucked the ribbon from his knee and twisted it about the blossoms. Then, still kneeling, he again presented them to the maiden. "Wilt thou not take them now, Penelope?"

"And I thank thee for them, Ezekiel," said the girl, as she bent forward. Again their eyes met, and again the young man felt the soft touch of her fingers; and as she took the flowers, one long braid of fair hair fell from her shoulder and rested upon his knee.

"Wilt thou not give me one back for a remembrance?" asked Ezekiel.

"Truly, if it would please thee, Ezekiel," was the answer; and selecting a fine spray of the blossoms, she fastened it in his collar. "But if thou givest me thy garter, what will take its place?"

"Wilt thou not give me this, Penelope?" he asked, seizing the ribbon which bound the girl's fair tress. She started with a slight cry and a blush, as if to detain him, but in a moment said, —

"Thou art bold, Ezekiel; yet now that thou hast the ribbon thou mayst keep it."

"I would, Penelope, that I might gain and keep thy heart so easily. Truly hearts are not given so readily as flowers and ribbons. But — Penelope — I have long loved thee. Oh, Penelope, Penelope, wilt thou not be my wife? In faith, my heart is bound as firmly in thy keeping as are thy flowers with the ribbon from my knee."

The young man still knelt, as when offering the flowers. His curling locks fell back upon his shoulders; his hands were outstretched toward the maiden; his face glowed with the intensity of his feelings. The girl shrank backward, clasping the flowers to her bosom, as if to check the beating of her heart. Her cheek paled for an instant. Then the rich hue deluged her face, her eyes dropped before Ezekiel's gaze, and she hid her sweet face among the blossoms.

"Thou wilt! thou wilt, dear Penelope!" exclaimed the youth joyfully, as he leaped to his feet and gently seized her hands. For an instant she glanced shyly from among the flowers, and then said softly, —

"Yes, Ezekiel, if the Lord will."

The robin leaped upon the topmost bough and twittered forth his song. The sunbeams danced upon the waters, and a gentle breeze stirred the budding branches of the forest. All Nature sang joyfully; and with her sang, in unison, the hearts of the youth and the maiden.

Chapter II.

TWO centuries and a half have passed since
Penelope and Ezekiel met thus in the
forest of Rocksbury. It was a quaint little
village which had within a half-dozen years
sprung up upon the peninsula of Shawmut, envi-
roned by the sea. There were few houses that
were pretentious. At the foot of the loftiest of
the three hills the people, in their settlement,
reserved a large open space for a common
ground, where cattle might range under proper
restrictions. At a little distance, but overlook-
ing the place reserved for a market-stead, they
built their meeting-house, — a rude structure,
with roughly hewn walls and roof of thatch.
The dwellings of the people, save it may be

one or two, were as rudely built, with such
materials as they might obtain from the forest.

Strange people were these. They lived in
huts upon the verge of the wilderness. They
drew their sustenance from the waters, or forced
it from the unwilling earth. They sang psalms,
and their lives were austere. It was the day of
small things in New England.

With perhaps a faint recognition of their
Norman ancestry, the settlers called their new
home Trimountaine, because of the three peaks
which overshadowed them. A year or two
later, one Isaac Johnson, a man of wealth and
much influence, with his wife, the beautiful
Lady Arbella, the daughter of an earl, came
among them. Their former home had been
in Boston in Old England. So great was the
respect which the people felt toward this excel-
lent man, and so much did they desire to do
honor to him and to his wife, that they resolved to discard the name of Trimountaine,
and to call their settlement Boston.

It was a great day for the colonists when a ship arrived, bringing fresh additions to their number. With the first appearance of a sail in the harbor, the news spread rapidly through the town; and the populace, of all ages and both sexes, flocked to the wharves to witness the arrival. There were men of grave demeanor and silver hair; sturdy young men, who had left their tasks undone, as if to perform a religious duty; matrons and maidens, decorous of speech and attire, but not a little attractive, despite their sombre gowns. All talked eagerly among themselves concerning the new-comers, and who and what they were, until the splash of the anchor was heard and the ship swung round at her moorings. Then a solemn hush fell over all. As the comers stepped upon the wharf they paused a moment, and with uncovered head, and face upraised, whispered a few words of thanksgiving and prayer. In a Roman Catholic country the on-lookers would have made quickly and silently the sign of the cross;

but these Puritans, abhorring the forms of Rome, stood in silence with bared heads, while the women folded their hands and reverently dropped their eyes upon the ground. Then calmly, but fervently, came the greetings of the people to the newly arrived. In those early days the governor deemed it not beneath the dignity of his station to be present amid the throng. His greetings were the first extended. When these had formally been made, and his deputy and assistants had also bidden the strangers welcome, the people crowded about with handshakings and cordial greetings, and with a thousand inquiries concerning matters political and religious in their old home across the sea.

Such was the scene upon the wharf in Boston upon a spring morning in the year 1635, five years before the occurrence in the forest of Rocksbury. It was the ship "Susan and Ellen" which swung at anchor on that morning. An unusually large number crowded the wharf upon this day, and no little commotion was created when, with unusual ceremony, Governor Haynes and his assistants arrived in a group together, and stood a little apart, watching the ship with interest.

"Why is his worship so bravely apparelled?" quoth one. "Doth he expect some person of note? Canst thou tell, John Mylom?"

"Hast not heard, Jacklin," replied Mylom, the cooper, as he twirled a heavy mallet in his hand, "that the honorable knight, Sir Richard Saltonstall, is expected by this ship? And I doubt me not that he will bring with him a goodly company. His worship, without doubt, comes hither to greet Sir Richard."

"Ay, goodman, I do now remember me," said Jacklin, the glazier.

At that moment the crowd parted, and a figure advanced clad wholly in black. A Geneva cloak covered his shoulders. His broad, square collar was of unusual whiteness, and the silver buckles upon his shoes were

polished with the greatest care. Upon his
head, in place of the hat with pointed crown,
he wore a closely fitting skull-cap of black silk.
His manner was solemn and dignified ; and as
the crowd made way, they all observed toward
him the greatest veneration. As he drew near
the group of magistrates, the same tokens of
respect were visible in those worthies.

"Good-morrow to thee, reverend sir," said
the governor.

"And to thee, also, worshipful sir," returned
the Reverend John Wilson.[2] "Thou, too, and
these honorable magistrates await friends from
the ship. I had but just now been warned
of her arrival, and hastened away, thinking it
meet that our friends should receive a proper
greeting."

"Yea, in truth," said the governor, "it were
well that so they should. Our last advices
concerning the coming of Sir Richard and his
company, as thou well knowest, foretold his
embarkation in the ship 'Susan and Ellen.'

Happy are we if so be Heaven hath so ordered it!"

At that moment Arthur Perry, the town-drummer,[3] leaped upon the cap-log of the wharf, with his drum upon his hip, and sent forth a rolling salute to the strangers. A dignified, martial figure appeared at the vessel's side, and carefully descended by the ladder of ropes to the boat, which tumbled and tossed with the tide below. He wore the same broad collar of white which adorned the shoulders of his friends upon the wharf. His tunic of dark brown was delicately embroidered with gold thread, and a sword, with hilt and scabbard elaborately wrought, hung at his side. His bared head disclosed his hair combed forward and clipped squarely across the forehead. His hands were covered with gauntlets of yellow leather.

When Sir Richard had entered the boat, he looked upward and saw, standing where he had stood, a stately lady. By her side was a

slighter form, that of a fair-haired girl of sixteen. We have seen her already, her form a
little fuller and more perfectly rounded, —
Penelope Pelham,[4] who five years later gathered
mayflowers in the forest of Rocksbury, and
there promised her love to Ezekiel Bolt.

The greetings of the governor and the lesser
magistrates to Sir Richard and his company
were warm, yet of great dignity. When these
were over, and Penelope had dropped her
modest courtesy, with her brother, John Pelham, who had accompanied her on the ship,
she entered a boat and proceeded at once to
a little settlement across the basin of the river
to which the colonists had given the name of
King Charles. This little settlement the home-
loving people had called Cambridge. Here,
upon the plantation of her brother, William
Pelham, Penelope found rest from her journey
and a home which she soon learned to love.
She roamed the forest freely, and penetrated
the wigwams of the savages, who were en-

chanted by her bright, sweet ways, while they wondered at her fair, soft skin and yellow hair. The Indians soon became her friends, and she had nothing to fear from them, as we have already heard her say to Ezekiel.

Chapter III.

"EZEKIEL," said Deputy-Governor Richard Bellingham, "I would have speech
with thee, this morning, upon a matter that
closely concerns me and thee also. Thou hast
been of my household these five years now
agone, and hast ever been faithful. Thou art
well conditioned among the people."

The deputy-governor hesitated for a moment, and cast a somewhat wistful glance at
his young secretary, as if to beseech him to
divine his meaning without further explana-
tion. But Ezekiel's face wore a puzzled look,
and Bellingham stirred the fire uneasily with
the long, brass-handled poker. It had never
occurred before that Ezekiel had seen the

deputy-governor ill at ease before him. But he waited for the mood to pass. In another moment Bellingham resumed : —

" I am the deputy-governor ; but why deputy? Am I not as wisely read and as well able to fill the governor's seat as Dudley?[5] I say this to thee in confidence, Ezekiel. But tell me, am not I as well thought of among the people as are Thomas Dudley and John Winthrop? What claim have they upon them that Bellingham hath not? Hast thou, Ezekiel, held speech among any of them concerning these things?"

" Nay, sir," answered Ezekiel; " but I have heard certain whisperings among them, to the end that thou shouldst be the governor, in Dudley's stead."

" Oh! sayest thou so, Ezekiel?" said the deputy, quickly. He gave the coals a final thrust, and then dropped the poker upon the hearth. It struck the stone with a sharp ring. The motion betrayed his agitation and

the unusual interest which the secretary's
communication had excited.

"But yet thou knowest that the General
Court hath much power over the people in
the choice of a chief magistrate," added the
secretary, fearing lest he had raised the hopes
of the deputy to too high a point.

"Yea, Ezekiel, the power of the magistrates is great among the people. But who
chooseth the magistrates themselves? The people! yea, the people! The time draweth near
when new deputies for the service of the General Court shall be chosen. Shall we not look
to it that true and godly men are chosen, who
will not fail to guide the people aright?"

"But how may this be done?"

"I must, forsooth, leave that with thee,
Ezekiel. Canst not thou, with thy persuasive
tongue and thy fluency of speech, make such
give ear to thee as have been admitted to
be freemen? But speak not to such of me,
nor of thy purpose. Mark out such men for

the office of deputy as thou art persuaded
will deal righteously. Talk then with such,
not as from me, nor as of a purpose, but
strive to learn and to guide their inclina-
tions. When thou art well satisfied, go
thou among the people where they most
often congregate. Canst thou not find many
at the ordinary of William Hudson?[6] Good
Master Hibbens, he who is the husband of
my sister Ann, will aid thee. Thou shouldst
gain also Nicholas Willys, the constable, for
he hath a goodly acquaintance.[7] Remember
Thomas Marshall, who hath the conduct of
the ferry to Winnisemett.[8] A garrulous fellow
he, and mayhap will do good service. Do
as best thou may, and I doubt me not that
righteous magistrates may be chosen. Teach
the people that the office of chief magistrate
should not rest with one man, year by year,
as hath too long been the case with Winthrop. I have heard speech to the end that
he should again be returned to the governor's

seat. But do thou as I have said, and right-
eousness shall prevail. When Richard Bellingham shall be the governor, then shall thy
reward come."

"'Troth, I would gladly do according to this
thy word, good sir," said the secretary. " But
I do it not for the desire of a reward. Thou
hast dealt kindly with me. But naught can
be said ill concerning the worthy Governor
Winthrop. To say aught ill would be but to
defeat our cause."

"Nay, Ezekiel, I would not have thee say
aught against his worship. He hath ever
filled his place right worthily. But he hath
filled a place of honor these many years, as
hath Dudley likewise. Why should not another
as worthy sit in the seat?"

"Why, truly? What may be done in the
fear of God shall be done soon, thou mayest
trust me for it," said Ezekiel.

As he spoke he drew from the pocket of
his tunic an ample handkerchief of homespun

linen. Unnoticed by him, a knot of sad-
colored ribbon fluttered down and fell upon
the rug at the deputy-governor's feet. It fell
at the moment when Bellingham, who had re-
gained his self-assurance during the conversation, stooped to recover the poker, which he
had dropped upon the hearth. He was in
a· remarkably good humor; for Ezekiel had
assented to his plans more readily than he
had feared would be the case. He was
therefore in a mood for rallying, and seizing the token he held it toward Ezekiel,
exclaiming, —

"How, now, Master Ezekiel? In truth I
had thought thou hadst no time for love-
making. But here, behold ·the favor of thy
fair mistress. Thou art artful, indeed."

Ezekiel was, for a moment, disconcerted,
but he soon recovered his composure.

"It is a matter," said the secretary,
gravely, "upon which I fain would seek
thy counsel."

The deputy-governor's manner instantly changed.

"Speak freely, my son," said he.

"The lady is Mistress Penelope Pelham, who dwelleth with her brother William, beyond the river."

"And hast thou proceeded far with her?"

"She hath, indeed, given to me her promise, with the ribbon from her hair."

"Then, forsooth, thou hast little need of counsel."

"Yea, but it were scarcely meet that I should take more important steps without thy consent."

"Mistress Pelham, thou sayest. Is it not she who came in company of Sir Richard?"

"The same, your worship. It is, her brother, Herbert, who hath in charge the moneys of the college across the river." [9]

"She hath a goodly reputation. She it is, with hair like unto gold, who sitteth oft with

Master Pelham and oft with Lady Saltonstall in the meeting-house."

"The same."

"From aught that I have heard thou canst do no better than to take her for thy wife. If it would do thee a service I will have discourse for thee with Master Pelham."

· "Nay, sir, but Master Pelham hath already been apprised of the affair, and hath graciously signified his approval."

"A good wife is of the Lord, my son. Thou hast done well in thy choosing. But bring her to me, that I may have discourse with her. I am exceeding lonely. My good wife, Elizabeth,[10] who came with me hither from Old Boston, is dead. Samuel, my son, hath returned to England.[11] Save thee and the others of my household, I am alone. Bring young Mistress Pelham hither, that her brightness may cheer this desolate room. I would fain assure her also of my regard for thee and her."

" Thou doest me too great honor, kind sir."

" But thou wilt fetch her? "

" If so be she will incline to my desire, and of this I give little doubt."

Who can measure the rapture of a young girl's mind, newly awakened to thoughts of love? It is then that the slightest wish of her lover is a law to her. Moreover, what young girl of the colony would not feel herself honored by the invitation of the deputy-governor to visit his mansion? It was with a beating heart that Penelope ascended the steps. It was one of the most pretentious of the dwellings of the colony, and stood upon the slope of Cotton Hill, the hill afterwards called Pemberton. It was built of brick imported from Holland, as was the old Province House, a few years later. When Mr. Bellingham first arrived in Boston, from Old Boston, in the year 1634, he purchased of Henry Symons, after being admitted an inhabitant, a dwelling upon the slope of what was then known as Cornhill, now the lower portion of Washington Street.[12]   Later he purchased a lot upon the eastern slope of Cotton Hill, and erected a fine mansion.   Across the highway, even then known as Tremont Street, was Boston's earliest burial-place, where, a century later, Sir Edmund Andros, the royal governor of the province, erected the first King's Chapel.

It was the steps of this mansion which Penelope ascended, in company with Ezekiel. The door swung open at the tap of the great brass knocker.   A black serving-man, clad in a livery of blue, wrought with silver lace, ushered the two into a wide hall panelled in dark oak.   At its extremity the oaken stairs ascended to a landing, where a wide arched window, with diamond-shaped panes of glass set in leaden sashes, gave light to the sombre hall.   A heavy curtain of rich crimson stuff checked the full flow of sunlight, and gave a roseate hue to that which entered. The walls were hung, after the ancient English fashion, with a long line of ancestral portraits, whose eyes glared forth from the dingy backgrounds and seemed to follow the young girl with their gaze. The great romancer tells us, too, of heavy carved furniture, a massive table, whereon rested a great pewter tankard, and upon the walls a suit of glittering armor.[18]

"His worship is above, Master Bolt," said the servant, "and awaits thy coming. Is it thy pleasure that I announce it?"

"Nay," answered Ezekiel. "We will go up at once."

The deputy-governor himself responded to the tap upon the door of his library, and bade Penelope a dignified but cheery welcome. He took both her hands in his, and with courteous grace led her to a great carved and cushioned chair before the fireplace. A glorious fire blazed upon the hearth, and reflected its glow upon the shining brazen fire-dogs and fender.

With his own hands the deputy-governor brought a footstool, and placed it beneath the young girl's feet. The action displayed the elegant lace ruffles about his wrists.

It did not escape Ezekiel's attention that the deputy had arrayed himself with more care than was his wont upon occasions of ordinary moment. In place of the gown and velvet cap which it was his custom to wear within his library, the magistrate was clad in his dress of ceremony. He wore a tunic of black velvet embroidered with gold, above which arose a broad ruff of white linen edged with costly lace. His small-clothes were likewise of black velvet, confined at the knee with buckles of gold. His stockings were of the finest and whitest of silk. The rosettes upon his shoes were freshly made. Even his dress-sword, worn only upon occasions of the greatest ceremony, lay upon the table, and the firelight gleamed upon the ruby in its hilt.

Penelope had never before beheld such
magnificence, save at a distance and upon
occasions of state.   A year before, when Captain Robert Keayne had first led forth the
Company of Artillery,[14] to do honor to the
chief magistrate, upon his investiture with his
office, she had seen such costly arrays.   But
among these stern people plainness of attire
was a rule of life.   For a time, therefore, the
girl could scarcely reply to the kind and flat-
tering words with which the deputy-governor
addressed her.   But the warmth of his greeting and his gentle manner soon aided her to
gain her self-possession.   This once effected,
the hour passed delightfully.   When, escorted
by Ezekiel, Penelope arose to take her leave,
the deputy-governor gracefully accompanied
her to the door of the apartment and dismissed her with a courtly bow.

"I pray, Master Ezekiel, may I not see
Mistress Pelham with thee here again? She
will ever be gladly welcome to my mansion."

The deputy-governor's urgent invitation was not unheeded. As the long winter closed in upon them, and the landscape grew dreary, when ice and snow lay upon the bay and in the forest, it was not uncommon for the passers-by to see a little drab-robed figure, always attended by Ezekiel, ascending the steps of the deputy-governor's mansion. Quite often, too, they caught a glimpse of a golden-haired young girl seated at the deeply embrasured windows, absorbed in her book or her embroidery. Once, indeed, a magistrate who came to consult the deputy-governor concerning a matter of grave import, heard the hum of the spinning-wheel and caught, through a half-open door, a gleam of golden hair and a glimpse of a white hand deftly twirling the thread.

" Pray, sir, whom hast thou below, so busy at her wheel? " inquired the magistrate. " I knew not that thou hadst so fair a guest within thy household."

"The young woman," answered the deputy-
governor, " is Mistress Pelham, who is ready to
be contracted to my secretary, Master Ezekiel
Bolt.   I have often urged her that she visit my
mansion, and she hath yielded graciously to my
desire.   Her presence hath wonderfully bright-
ened this lonely household.   But she cometh
but for an hour, or to perform some gentle
act of kindness, even as thou hast seen.   I
have greatly urged that Ezekiel will yet abide,
together with his wife, beneath my roof, when
they shall at length be made one flesh."

"And will this soon occur? "

"Nay, I have not had speech with Ezekiel
of late concerning that point.   But the bans
will be published soon."

The deputy but told what had long been
of common speech among the gossips of the
colony.   There was no surprise when, a few
weeks later, the Rev. Mr. Wilson arose in the
meeting-house, with a demeanor even more
grave than was his wont.   Young men and

maidens, old men and the aged women seated in the fore seat grew attentive, as he drew from the psalm-book a folded paper. Slowly unfolding, he read, —

"Marriage is intended between Ezekiel Bolt, of this town, and Penelope Pelham, of Cambridge ; and this is the first publication of the bans."

Chapter IV.

THE winter passed slowly, but it seemed none too long to Ezekiel. He was burdened with a heavy care which Bellingham had laid upon him. He was totally unaccustomed to political intrigue. Yet he was only too glad to do what lay within his power honorably to further the interests of his patron. He diligently but cautiously canvassed the town, chatting with fishermen upon the wharves, with the groups which gathered in the public house kept by William Hudson, with the ferryman, Thomas Marshall, who, like many of his kind, kept himself acquainted with the gossip of the town, and fulfilled many of the purposes of a daily newspaper. They were an unsuspicious people, and political parties in local affairs were unknown among them. It is not surprising then that, little by little, a sentiment arose among the people favorable to the promotion of Bellingham from the position of deputy-governor to that of chief magistrate of the colony. His entire familiarity with public affairs, his education and social position, his dignified manners, each was urged by his adherents. Each of these imagined himself to have been the originator of the idea of Bellingham's advancement. So skilfully had Ezekiel managed the affair, that no whisper was afloat that Bellingham himself had been the father of the thought, and that public opinion was being formed by his shrewd secretary. To be sure, a slight hauteur in the deputy-governor's manner and a somewhat overbearing nature had not, in the past, added to his popularity as a citizen. But all this appeared to be forgotten, for surely none could be more genial in his every-day intercourse with his fellow-men. His air was as balmy as the spring-time. If there was a slight chill beneath this warmth, if there was a certain grimness in the smile when its brightness had faded, it was either unnoticed or ascribed to his well-known austerity. He was ever ready with a cheery word for rich or poor. Even the children were not overlooked, but were greeted with a thawed-out smile, a pat of the head, or a present of a penny. In certain cases, in which the father of the child so honored chanced to be a man of some influence among his fellows, the gratuity reached the sum of sixpence. Mothers with children in their arms were complimented upon the beauty of their offspring. Elderly ladies were greeted with earnest inquiries concerning their health, and went away impressed with the courtliness and dignity of the deputy-governor. Always attentive upon the stated religious exercises, he relaxed none of his vigilance in this regard. He was even more punctual than

ever in his attendance upon the weekly lecture
and the public services on Sunday. Once or
twice his voice was heard in chanting the
psalm, although he had not before been accustomed to join in this exercise. He was often
seen to drop a jingling coin into the poor-box.
Now and then a pumpkin from his garden was
sent, in manner perhaps unnecessarily public,
to some poor widow, or a bottle of wine was
sent from his cellar to an invalid. This latter,
indeed, he always carried and presented in
person, with many assurances of sympathy;
and in his homeward walk he never failed to
mention his visit to some one whom he met,
quite incidentally, to be sure. Subscription
papers upon matters of private charity or of
public interest never failed to receive his signature, with a generous sum against it.

A rap was heard one day upon the great
knocker of the deputy-governor's mansion. A
man of unusually dignified mien was escorted
at once to the library upon the floor above.

The deputy-governor glanced up from his desk, where he was engaged in carefully computing his chances of obtaining the governorship, from some data furnished by Ezekiel. A generous smile overspread his features as he recognized his visitor. But as he rose to greet him the deputy-governor did not forget to place the paper, upon which he had been making his computation, safely beyond the reach of possible scrutiny. The deputy-governor was careful about these little matters.

"Thou art well come, Master Maud," said the deputy-governor, as he extended his hand. "It is long since this pleasure has been mine, and yet thou art my nearest neighbor."

"Verily, thou sayest truly, worshipful sir. Yet it hath been no unfriendliness, but thy engrossment in public affairs, that hath made me seem to be unneighborly. But it hath been borne upon me to-day to have speech with thee upon a matter that doth greatly concern the public weal," said Daniel Maud.

"Sayest thou so, Master Maud? I pray what is this weighty matter?"

"It hath been thought needful that a school be established in the town, at which the children of all the people may be taught without price. It hath been decided that the inhabitants most greatly blessed in worldly goods shall be sought of, that they may contribute to this end, according to their ability."

"A wise course, Master Maud, and one which I do heartily commend. The more wise is it, if so be it that thou shalt be chosen to be the master thereof."

"Such hath been the intent of those who have been the leaders in the matter," said Master Maud, with Puritan directness.

"It is well," said the deputy-governor. "And now, good sir, hast thou already some assurances?"

"Yea, verily, the governor, likewise good Master Winthrop, have each given his promise in the sum of ten pounds."

"More, forsooth, than I can well afford. Yet I will add according to my fortune," said the deputy-governor. "Hast thou here the scroll? Shall it be forty shillings?"

"As thou wilt, good sir," answered the schoolmaster.

The deputy-governor placed his signature beneath the others.[15]

"I will give thee the money at once," said he, opening a secret drawer. "It were well that this matter were wholly completed." He handed his visitor two broad pieces of gold. The schoolmaster placed them with others in his purse, which hung at his belt, but uttered no word of thanks. He sat a moment, as if in thought. Finally he spoke : —

"I had thought to hold speech with thee concerning yet one thing more ; yet I know not if it be well."

Bellingham looked at Maud inquiringly. He surmised at once that the subject uppermost in the schoolmaster's mind was that which had now grown to be the chief topic of the town; yet he was far too crafty to assist the school-master in solving the doubt which was in his thought as to the proprieties of the occasion. None should be able to say that Bellingham had sought to be elevated to the chief magis-tracy. It was not that the deputy-governor shrank from seeking office. He had no con-scientious scruples upon this point. But he wished not to seem to seek it; he wished that his election might appear to be spontaneous, the general uprising of an enthusiastic people. In short, he had "placed himself in the hands of his friends." And so he craftily waited for Maud himself to broach the subject. He maintained the same inquiring, somewhat mys-tified, expression which he assumed at Maud's remark. Guileless himself, the schoolmaster could not fancy dissimulation in others. Hence he regarded Bellingham's affectation of igno-rance of his purpose as undoubtedly genuine. Had a doubt of this overshadowed his mind,

the mental shock would have closed his lips.
But no such catastrophe occurred, and Maud
continued : —

"I have heard much speech among the
people of late, worshipful sir, to the end
that thou shouldst be the follower of Thomas
Dudley, in the governor's seat. I know not if
this be more than idle gossip, yet I am persuaded there existeth a strong desire that this
should come to pass."

"Sayest thou so?" asked Bellingham. The
expression of his face instantly changed from
that of inquiry to one of intense surprise.
"Indeed, sir, my secretary, Master Bolt, hath
informed me that such speech hath been heard
among those who frequent the public house.
But the speech of idlers hath little weight."

"Nay, sir, it is not alone the speech of
idlers. Many who are deemed men of wisdom approve this thing. Nay, indeed, I also
approve it," said Daniel Maud, his directness
of speech again asserting itself. The look of

surprise had gradually melted away, and in its place appeared an expression of undisguised satisfaction.

"Thou art over kind, good Master Maud," said the dissembler; "yet I scarce count myself worthy to sit in the seat which Haynes and Vane and Winthrop have filled so worthily, not to mention the worshipful Governor Dudley, who hath well pleased the people."

"Others may judge of thy fitness. But I pray thou wilt not refuse, if so be it that thou art called to be the governor!"

The deputy-governor did not reply for a moment, and seemed to be lost in deep thought.

"I will answer thee frankly," he said at length, "even as thy speech has been plain with me. Thou knowest that I do not seek advancement. I fain would be a follower rather than a leader of men. Yet I would not shrink from serving the people. Far be it from me that I should shrink from that."

"It is well, then," said the schoolmaster, rising. "It hath been asked of me, being thy nearest neighbor, if, in my belief, thou wouldst accept the trust. I may say, then, that thou wilt do even according as the people will."

"Even so, good Master Maud."

The schoolmaster, without further ceremony, withdrew, and left Bellingham alone and wrapped in thought. Whether it was the result of this conference, or by some other means, it would be difficult at this day to determine; but it is quite certain that a rumor of the deputy-governor's humility, of his reluctance to assume grave responsibilities, but of his willingness to serve the people, became current, and greatly increased his already wide-spread popularity. Some indeed ventured the suspicion, quite unreasonable of course, that his humility, so suddenly born, would not be lasting, and that beneath the remarkable affability lurked a manner of thought and mind quite at variance with the outward appearance. But none of these cavillers could, when confronted, give a valid reason for his suspicions.

A sentiment arose, too, looking toward a frequent rotation in the office of governor. Many feared that the too frequent placing of one man in the office of chief magistrate would tend toward the establishment of a life-tenure of the office. A strong feeling also arose favorable to a return of Winthrop to the chief seat for yet another term. So day by day the controversy waxed warmer and warmer.

Chapter V

IT was on a bright May morning that Nicholas Willys, the constable, bearing his badge of office, knocked at the door of every freeman of the town,[16] and gave due warning that upon that day week the election would be held of deputies to represent the town in the General Court. The announcement created unusual interest; for now the question of Bellingham's advancement to the governor's seat would, in a degree at least, be solved. As time had passed, the ardor of some of his less strong adherents had somewhat cooled, and that of the friends of Winthrop had correspondingly increased. A slight feeling of distrust had, in some inexplicable manner, crept in among certain of the people. But they were of the class whose influence was not the greatest in the community. There were few, indeed, whose opposition to the movement was outspoken and earnest. These contented themselves with urging that the present deputies to the General Court should be returned. It was argued that none could fill the position with greater distinction than had Captain Edward Gibones. As for William Tynge, was not he the treasurer of the town's funds, and as such should not he sit in the General Court and care for the town's interests?

Those who still maintained their adherence to Bellingham owned that William Tynge should, indeed, be returned to his seat in the General Court. Concerning him there was no dispute; but they could see in William Hibbens qualities which betokened his great superiority to Captain Gibones in statesmanship.

To one who gave the subject thought, it soon
appeared quite evident that William Hibbens,
whose wife was the sister of the deputy-governor, might surely be relied upon to advance
the interests of his brother-in-law; but Captain Gibónes, it was suspected, would be
content that Bellingham should remain the
deputy-governor for yet another term. Indeed,
the captain had been heard to say, a little
incautiously perhaps, that although Mr. Dudley had filled the deputy-governor's chair for
three successive terms, he had only that very
year been advanced to the foremost place.
It was true that Haynes and Vane had each
held the governor's office for but a single
year; but Winthrop had often been called
to the governor's seat. If Dudley should be
dropped, he asked, after a single term in the
chief magistracy, would not the action reflect
upon his capacity, or possibly even upon his
integrity? These were matters, Captain Gibones had been heard to say, that it would

be well to consider. Such being the sentiments of the captain, it was urged, both quietly and openly, that it would be far preferable to send Mr. Hibbens to fill his seat at the General Court.

When, at length, the day of the election arrived, the whole town was astir. It appeared much like a *fête* day, for many were present from the adjoining towns. Throughout the colony the same interest was manifest, and the streets of Boston were filled with the free-men. Even before the tap of Arthur Perry's drum was heard in the streets, they were all abroad and eagerly discussing the great question of the day. Seldom had the market-stead seen so great and so earnest a company of citizens congregated together. Many were clustered about the little thatched meeting-house, and around the scaffold, whipping-post, and pillory, which stood beneath its eaves. There was Captain Robert Keayne, a martial figure, whose house fronted upon the market-

stead. Beside the church was the dwelling
of Robert Scott, the color-bearer in Captain
Keayne's Company of Artillery. He, too, came
forth, and leaning upon the low paling, about
which twined great clusters of morning-glory
vines, talked earnestly with the by-standers.
From across the way came Valentine Hill,
the merchant, arm-in-arm with his next-door
neighbor, Anthony Stoddard, the linen-draper.
Francis Lysle, the barber, had opened his shop
an hour earlier than was his wont, but had
closed it hastily, leaving the great key pro-
jecting from the lock, as he saw the gathering
in the market-stead. He reasoned, and truly,
that none would demand his service while the
interest was so great without.

Here, in a group, were Henry Messenger
and Sergeant John Davis, from the pockets
of both of whom projected carpenters' rules;
John Newgate, the hatter, and Thomas Savage,
the tailor. Richard Parker came forth from
his house beside the jail, and with his neigh-

bors, Richard Tuesdale and John Leverett, walked briskly down Queen Street, to the market-stead. William Hudson, the innkeeper, deemed it not prudent to close his tap-room, for the thirsty ones would call often during the day. And so he stood upon the porch of his inn,[17] just at the foot of the market-place, with his hands upon his hips, and softly intoned a psalm, in consonance with the creaking of the sign which swung in the breeze overhead, or chatted with his neighbor, William Davies, the elder. John Cogan was in close converse with Captain Edward Gibones, across their garden pales, and later the two sauntered out together and joined the throng. Here, too, amid the crowd, were Henry Webb, and John Ruggles, and William Davies, the younger, and William Pierce, and David Sellick; and here was Robert Nash, wearing a frock besmeared with the blood of kine.

Lewis Kidby with William Kirkby and Waters Sinnott had been up with the early

5

dawn, casting their lines in the outer harbor. The wind was blowing fresh and strong from the southeast, and Kidby's little shallop skimmed merrily over the waves, and came up into the wind, off the wharf of Edward Tyng. The killock splashed from the bow, and the little vessel swung around by the head. In another moment the sail rattled down. The three men sprang upon the deck, and hurriedly clewed down the canvas. Then they carefully lowered a large basket of fish into the row-boat, which they had left fastened to a float, sprang in after it, and pulled ashore with sturdy strokes. Kirkby and Sinnott handled the oars, while Kidby stood in the stern and gazed up King Street, at the fast-gathering crowd in the market-stead. In a moment the boat grounded upon the beach near Hudson's ordinary. The three fishermen hastily sprang on shore, drew the boat high upon the beach, and secured it to a large bowlder. With their basket of fish in hand they entered the side door of the

inn, which opened upon the water side, and
tramped heavily through the hall to the tap-
room. It was empty.

"What, ho!" shouted Kidby, as he pounded
the floor with his heavy fishing-boot. "Where
art thou, Master Hudson?"

"Here am I," answered Hudson, from without, as he left off chatting with Davies, the
gunsmith, and hastened within. "Pray, why
this clatter? Ah! is it thou, Kidby?" he said,
as, entering the tap-room, he caught sight of
the group of fishermen. "And you, too, Sinnott and Kirkby? What luck to-day?"

Sinnott pushed forward the basket with one
foot, as he leaned with his back against the
bar, on which he supported himself with both
elbows.

"In faith, we would all be in better humor
an we heard the sound of the skillet," said
Kirkby.

"That thou shalt hear quickly, an it please
thee," said Hudson. He selected three of the

finest of the fish, and strode down the long hall toward the kitchen.

"Look thee, Priscilla," they heard him call out. "Three hungry men beyond, and a fish for each. Make thee haste, girl!" Then they heard his heavy tread returning. "Thy humor shall be bettered soon," quoth the innkeeper, as he re-entered the tap-room. "Meanwhile a glass of our neighbor Tyng's last brewing will aid thy appetite."

"My appetite needs no aid," said Kidby, "and I doubt me not my brothers are like minded; yet to test the new brew would not be amiss."

"Ay! so say we," said the others, as the three seated themselves at a table in a corner of the tap-room. "Sit thou with us, Master Hudson."

"An it please thee, I will," said the innkeeper, as he placed upon the table a large pewter tankard overflowing with ale. "I can give thee wine, if it would please thee better," he continued, looking at Kidby, as he seemed to be the leader of the party. "But yesterday John Viall, the vintner, placed a fresh butt in my cellar. John Mylom is even now below, making tight the hoops," he added, as the sound of blows was heard beneath the floor.

"Nay, the beer is better for hungry men," answered Kidby. As he poured out a foaming mugful and lifted it to his lips, Priscilla entered, holding high a platter from which came a savory odor.

"Done to a turn," exclaimed Sinnott, now speaking for the first time. "Thou art well deserving a good husband, fair Mistress Priscilla."

"Let thou not seek me, then," retorted the girl.

"Ha ! ha !" laughed Kirkby, while the others joined boisterously. "The lass hath a sharp tongue."

"That she hath," admitted Sinnott, a little sheepishly. Then all were silent until hunger was satisfied.

Glancing up as they heard a step on the threshold, they saw the sturdy form of Davies, the gunsmith, whose chat with the landlord without had been broken by the entrance of the fishermen.

"Is it thoú, Davies?" said Kirkby, tilting the tankard forward and peering into its depths. "A good mugful left, and more in the cask below. Drink thee, man, and drink we all to the king."

"The king! Long live the king!" said all, springing to their feet, raising their mugs aloft, then draining them to the dregs.

"And now," asked Sinnott, with a little of impatience in his tone, "how go on the matters in the town?"

"Ay," rejoined Kidby; "how goeth the talk? Who shall be the governor?"

"Troth," answered Hudson, "ye are in good time. The vote hath not yet been taken."

"Yea," said Kirkby, eagerly, "we did hasten homeward. But how goeth the speech of the people?"

"Thou knowest," answered Davies, "that six days now agone the people of the town did choose for service of the General Court Mr. Treasurer Tyng, and in place of Captain Gibones, Master William Hibbens. The freemen of the town did also choose that Master Bellingham should be one of those who should order the town's occasions for the year next ensuing." [18]

"Ay," interrupted Sinnott; "thou didst not think that we had been upon a voyage to Plymouth?"

"Peace, Sinnott!" expostulated Kidby.— "Thou art minded, Master Davies, that Master Bellingham will be given the foremost place to-day?"

"Nay, that I cannot say. Truly it doth so portend; but there be many who say that Master Winthrop should be once more made the governor. Yet others greatly fear lest he should be brought to believe such to be his right."

"In truth," said Kirkby, "I do fear as much. We want no governor for life."

"Nay, that we do not," exclaimed Hudson. "My voice is all for Master Bellingham."

"Nay! nay! I like it not, I like it not," said Kidby, with much feeling. "The good people of Rocksbury will like it not. The men of Boston have held the governor's seat from the beginning, until a twelvemonth since, when Thomas Dudley was advanced from the deputy-governor's chair. His townsmen will not willingly consent that he shall so soon be displaced."

"But why dost thou not like it?" demanded Hudson.

"We are accustomed to deal plainly with one another," said Kidby in reply, "we hide nothing; yet if I do not mistake me, the worshipful deputy-governor doth wear a mask. It hath not been his custom in the past to greet me in the public streets. Nay, I scarce thought that he knew my name. And yet, but

a week agone, he greeted me at the spring-gate, and asked of my luck at fishing and begged that I would sell him a fine cod, which I had caught that morning. Oh! his worship is a sly fellow."

"Yea, grant that he hath cunning, but all the more may he be fit to care for the people's good," urged Sinnott.

"But I would not that Richard Bellingham should think my eyes darkened by his flattery," persisted Kidby. "Will he buy yet another cod from my hand when he shall be the governor? Nay, verily. He will then be the great Governor Bellingham in his velvet; I, but poor Lewis Kidby, the fisherman, in fustian."

"Nay, I think not so meanly of his worship," said Kirkby.

"Thou shalt see," retorted Kidby; "thou shalt see. But let us go and listen to the people." And they mingled with the throng in the market-stead.

During this conversation at Hudson's ordinary, the deputy-governor's secretary pushèd his way slowly through the throng. He stopped here and there amid the crowd, chatting a moment with a friend or neighbor and having a cheery word for all. Public opinion might be divided, to some extent, in its estimate of the deputy-governor's character. Concerning that of Ezekiel there was no variance ; he was regarded as a friend by all. As the deputy-governor had said, he was well conditioned among the people. He had a smile for all whom he met. Now, as he emerged from the throng on the further side of the market-stead, the figure of a girl attracted his eye, as she walked in the garden of the Rev. John Wilson, and he at once approached the paling.

"Penelope ! "

"Ezekiel ! is it thou?" said the girl ; and a look of pleasure overspread her face.

"I thought not to see thee to-day, Penelope," said Ezekiel.

"But thou art not sorry?" said the girl, as she slipped her hand in his, across the low paling of the garden.

"Dost thou remember a year agone?" whispered Ezekiel.

"It did sweeten my dreams, last night,— the thought of it," she said softly; "and as I gathered these flowers in the pastor's garden, I bethought me of my dream and of the flowers that thou didst gather for me."

"Thou didst give me for the paltry flowers a gift beyond all price, Penelope."

"But thy heart was given with the flowers," she said.

"In truth, Penelope, my heart, my life! Thy love is the well-spring in my heart. Let that fail and all is dust and ashes. My cares have been grievous these weeks past, as thou hast seen. Too little have I seen of thee. But thy smile hath cheered my anxious hours. Let us hope to-day may end the weightiest cares. Already success portends. His worship said to me, not once, but many times, 'When Bellingham shall be the governor, then shall thy reward come.' Heaven knows that I have but done my duty, and for my love of him. But only yesternight he did urge that we be married soon, and that we take up our abode within his mansion. In truth he hath sent advices to workmen in England, that they forward at the earliest day furnishings fit, indeed, for a governor's bride."

"His worship is indeed kind," said Penelope, an even unwonted softness coming into her eyes.

"And shall it not be as Governor Bellingham saith?"

"Even as he saith, if the Lord will," said Penelope, softly.

The pressure of the hands, hidden among the morning-glory vines, grew stronger for an instant. Then, as footsteps approached, the pressure loosened; and looking into each other's eyes, the young man and maiden parted. As Ezekiel turned away he saw that the great clusters of blue and white blossoms which had covered the paling had faded while they talked.

Chapter VI.

L ARGER and more earnest grew the crowd
in the market-stead, and some in the
throng were even contentious. The adherents
of Bellingham had fully believed that success
would readily perch upon their banners; but
it soon became apparent there was a strong
influence favorable to the re-election of Winthrop, and it was made no secret that this
influence was exerted by the members of the
General Court. Indeed, the opposition from
this quarter was violent. The people, on the
other hand, who declined to be influenced
by the magistrates, clung to Bellingham as
their candidate. So the contention in the

market-stead grew stronger and the hubbub greater, until the tap of the drum was again heard in the street. Then a murmur ran through the crowd, and cries of: "The governor! the governor!" The crowd parted, the people forming a lane through the centre of the market-stead. Still was heard the steady tap of the drum, and then through the throng came Captain Robert Keayne, in full regimentals, carrying at his shoulder his long, heavy sword, with its iron hilt. Behind him came his company of artillery, their burnished halberds flashing in the sunlight. In the midst marched Robert Scott, sturdy of form, and bearing aloft the blood-red flag of England, of a deeper hue than the scarlet coats which the soldiers wore.

In a moment the murmurs of admiration which ran through the crowd were hushed, and as the form of Captain Keayne and the foremost of his men disappeared within the door of the meeting-house, the dignified Governor

Dudley appeared. With him walked Deputy-Governor Bellingham, upon whose appearance a slight murmur arose, which was as quickly hushed. Behind them walked alone the Rev. Nathaniel Ward, formerly of the church at Ipswich, who was to deliver the annual election sermon. Then followed eight men of dignified bearing, walking two and two. These were the honorable Court of Assistants. At their head walked John Winthrop, a slender man with auburn hair and thin beard and mustache. His eyes were brown and large and lustrous. He was habited wholly in black velvet. Beside him walked Sir Richard Saltonstall, dressed much as we saw him a few years ago, as he stepped from the deck of the "Susan and Ellen." The same elegant sword hung at his side, and betrayed his knightly rank. After these came Dudley and Humfrey, John Winthrop the younger, Bradstreet, and Stoughton; and at the last came Increase Nowell, who for many years had been the much respected secretary of the General Court. Then came the deputies of the towns, thirty-four in number, headed by Tyng and Hibbens, the deputies for Boston.

When all these had passed into the meeting-house, the people followed. At the door, as they passed, · stood the secretary, bearing a large basket, into which each of the freemen dropped, as he entered, a slip of paper, upon which he had indicated his choice for governor and deputy-governor. There were many whose duties at home would not permit of absence to attend the General Court of Elections. Such had sent their proxies by the hands of others, and these were received as if the parties themselves were present.

The meeting-house was speedily filled with the freemen, for the interest was great, and there were many wandering thoughts as the preacher wound through the length of his election sermon.[19] This was plainly intended to conciliate, if possible, the two contending elements in the colony, — the magistrates, with their aristocratic tendencies, and the people, with their growing hatred of long tenures of office. At length the sermon was over. A sigh escaped many of those present. A deep silence fell upon all, as the preacher took his seat. Then the governor arose in his place upon the platform, advanced a step or two, and laid his hand impressively upon the Bible.

"Magistrates, deputies, freemen," he said earnestly, "may we all take these words to our souls. Give ear, now, that the honorable secretary may announce to us the votes."

A still deeper hush fell upon the assemblage as the governor resumed his seat. Increase Nowell, the secretary, placed the basket containing the ballots upon a large table which had been brought in for the purpose. As he did so, Robert Scott advanced, bearing the flag, and took his position by the table, overshadowing it with the crimson folds. For a time no sound was heard save the rustle of the ballots, as they were swiftly counted. Presently the secretary advanced, and amid a deathlike stillness announced, —

"The General Court of Elections hath chosen to be the governor, for the year ensuing, Master Richard Bellingham, he having, in the numbering of the votes, six more than the others. The court hath also chosen to be the deputy-governor, Master John Endicott."

A sound as of a long-drawn sigh swelled through the meeting-house. Then a voice broke the stillness.

"Behold, sirs," said the voice, "I have not yet given in my vote, and there are divers others of my fellows by me, who likewise have not given theirs. May not we, forsooth, have our liberty?"

A murmur at once arose, which was checked in a moment, as the venerable Bradstreet arose and addressed the governor and the court.

"Nay, sirs," he said; "it hath been made an order of the magistrates that at courts of

elections the freemen shall give in their votes
at the ' doors. These who now claim their
liberty have not obeyed this order of the
magistrates. Wherefore, then, should they
claim their liberty?"

.So also said Stoughton and Humfrey. But
the Winthrops kept silence.[20]

The solemn oaths were taken by the newly
elected governor and deputy. Then forth went
the people into the market-stead once more;
and as they went forth and filled the place,
a confused sound of voices arose, which at
the first disturbed the august deliberations of
the General Court within.

"I tell thee, as I told thee before, I like it
not," said Kidby, the fisherman, as he paused
beneath the shadow of the pillory. He spoke
a little excitedly; and Davies, the gunsmith,
whom he addressed, paused beside him, while
a crowd instantly clustered about the two.

"Nay, but we cannot always have all things
to our minds," answered the gunsmith. " In

truth, I would gladly see Thomas Dudley once more in the governor's seat. But yet would it not be better that Bellingham should sit there than that Winthrop should claim his perpetual right?"

"Ay! that be true," said a voice in the crowd. "Didst not see that both the elder and the younger Winthrop held their peace, when the belated ones claimed their liberty in the election? They could not openly insist that the votes should be admitted, forsooth, for I give little doubt that they would have borne the name of Winthrop."

"Truth!" exclaimed another. "Mark well that Bellingham hath now his election by but six votes. Had those who claimed their liberty but been admitted, the speech of the people might have been different now."

"Peace, men!" said Richard Parker, elbowing his way through the throng. "His worship Governor Bellingham is the people's friend. He hath little sympathy with the lordly

ways of our magistrates, and will look to the
people's rights.   There will be heard no more
of magistrates for life."   ,

"And the magistrates and the court have
little sympathy with him, good brother Parker,"
shouted John Leverett from the outermost
edge of the throng.

"Why sayst thou so?" asked Parker.

"Hast not heard," said Leverett, "that no
sooner had the people gone forth, than the
General Court did vote to retract the order
of the last court, whereby the sum of one
hundred pounds should be paid annually to
his worship the governor?"[21]

A startled look was visible upon all faces,
and Kidby answered, —

"The Court, then, hath declared open war-
fare with Bellingham.   War it may be.   I
trow that within the twelvemonth his worship
will be at war with the people as well.   He
will no more greet me at the spring-gate and
buy a fresh cod at my hand."

" Peace, good brother Kidby !" said Parker.
" Be not thou a prophet of evil. I'll warrant thee that Governor Bellingham will yet,
ere the twelvemonth passes, make thee his
friend, even though he may not buy thy cod."

" Nay," answered Kidby, " I care not if
he buy the cod or no. I only ask that he
trample not on the people's rights."

The throng broke, and scattered here and
there about the town. The three fishermen
sauntered down to the beach to look to the
moorings of their boat. They had not thought
to go forth again that day; but when they
reached the beach the wind was fair and the
sun had not yet ceased to cast a westward
shadow; and so, with a parting mug of ale
at Hudson's ordinary, they once more weighed
anchor, and turned their shallop's prow toward
the outer harbor, as they chanted a psalm in
unison.

Chapter VII.

WE last saw Ezekiel Bolt as he pressed the hand of Penelope across the palings of the Rev. Mr. Wilson's garden. He glanced backward for an instant as he was about to plunge into the crowd in the market-stead, and caught a gleam of fair hair and the wave of a white hand. The hours which followed were momentous to him. He was anxious for the success of his patron, for his patron's sake; and although he could not believe that, in the event of failure, Mr. Bellingham would relax his interest in him and his suit, still nothing could be more natural than that a successful candidate would be more willing to aid his friends than one whom fortune had not so favored. It was then with a feeling of mingled relief and exultation that Ezekiel, who had stood near the door of the church during the long sermon and the subsequent solemnities, heard the announcement of Increase Nowell. Slipping through the throng at the door, he did not await the final ceremonies, but sped across the market-stead and hastily entered the pastor's gateway. As he reached forth his hand to lift the shining brass knocker, the door opened and the dignified minister stood upon the threshold.

"What news, my good Ezekiel, from the General Court of Elections?" he demanded eagerly. For some years the Rev. John Wilson had been selected by the magistrates to preach the election sermon; but this year the freemen, in the contest which had lately arisen between them and the magistrates, had insisted upon their right to select the election preacher. Mr. Wilson, unwilling to bring him-

self into conflict with the people, especially
in a matter purely political, had advised the
magistrates to yield to the pressure thus brought
upon them. And so it came about that the
young preacher, Nathaniel Ward, who had
left Ipswich under a slight cloud, was selected
as the preacher, in response to the popular
demand. It was not, then, strange that Mr.
Wilson, unwilling, perhaps, to embarrass the
young preacher by his presence, had kept
aloof from the Court of Elections.

"The magistrates and the freemen, sir,"
answered Ezekiel, "have chosen good Master
Bellingham to the first place in the colony,
and have also chosen Master John Endicott
to be the deputy-governor."

As Ezekiel uttered these words, a joyful
exclamation was heard at the extremity of
the hall, and Penelope glided forward. Later
Ezekiel remembered and regretted that he
had not noticed Mr. Wilson's remark, in
comment upon his announcement.

" Enter, Ezekiel," said Mr. Wilson, the instinct of hospitality at once asserting itself. " Mistress Penelope will yet tarry for a time with us."

" Nay, sir," said Penelope, " thou art kind, but truly I must hasten homeward. Already is the sun high in the heavens, and I gave my promise to my brother Herbert that I would not tarry beyond the declaration, that I might acquaint him with it."

" He did not, then, come to the Court of Elections?"

" Nay, sir. He was detained by divers weighty matters, and did send by my hand his proxy. This I did pass to Master Hibbens, and came at once hither."

" And how wilt thou return to Newtowne?"

" As I came, forsooth, in my canoe," said Penelope, laughing.

The two young people bade adieu to the pastor. Avoiding the groups of men who still stood about the market stead and in front of

the meeting-house, they walked slowly up
Queen Street, past the jail, built of heavy
hewn logs, and turned up Tremont Street.
Thence they wandered past the burying-
ground, where the gentle Lady Arbella Johnson had been laid to rest, and so reached
the Centry Field. Slowly they wandered
through the shaded lanes and across the sweet
meadow to the river-bank. Here, beneath
the shadow of Fox Hill, they found Penelope's
canoe moored to a tree.

"And what thinkest thou of the result?"
asked Penelope, as, with two or three strong
strokes, she sent the canoe skimming lightly
over the water. Ezekiel sat in the bow of
the canoe facing the girl, and dabbled the
fingers of one hand lightly in the water as
they sped along.

"In troth," answered Ezekiel, a little
soberly, "it were impossible that I should not
be gratified that Master Bellingham is chosen.
But yet I have heard some things in the

market-stead to-day which have made me think."

" Pray, what has thou heard?" asked the girl, anxiously. "Surely nothing that concerns thee and me."

" Nay, Penelope, nothing that concerns thee. But the speech of the people hath been exceeding plain concerning Governor Bellingham. Some have said that while he doth pretend to care greatly for the people, his care is only for himself."

"Oh, I cannot believe that such is the manner of his worship. He hath ever been so kind to thee and to me."

"Yes, he hath been kind to both of us."

"And think, too," urged Penelope, "how the General Court did add him to the committee on military affairs, and did give them power to imprison or to put to death such as they judge to be enemies of the commonwealth."

" I do remember. It was the same year

in which thou and I came hither from across the sea, and I marvelled much that such great power should be delegated by the General Court. But none hath ever said that Master Bellingham hath unworthily discharged that great trust. Why, then, certain of the people have lost their faith in him, I cannot say. Kidby, the fisherman, hath done much to foment this discontent. I own frankly that I would greatly wish that his worship the governor had won his place by more than six votes."

"Trouble not thyself," said the girl, gayly. "He will make himself so greatly beloved that if it please God that he be spared until another year, he will be elected by many more than six votes."

"Let us trust so, Penelope," said Ezekiel, drawing forth his handkerchief and drying his dripping fingers. "But I fear me greatly. When once the people have gained a belief, it is not easy to turn them to another."

"'Thou art gloomy," said Penelope. "'Thou hast forgotten that our own happiness is now assured."

"Forgotten it, Penelope!" cried the young man. "Nay, be not offended at my mood. How canst thou say so; when I did come at once to thee, when the declaration was made?"

"Thou didst so, Ezekiel. But thou knowest not how a woman's heart looketh eagerly toward the future."

"Thou shamest me in reminding me of it, dear Penelope. But believe me, my own heart did bound, when I knew that success had come; for I felt that now, at last, I could claim thee. May Heaven forgive me if I thought of my own and not of my master's weal!"

"Heaven will forgive thee, do thou never fear."

"And now, Penelope," said Ezekiel, as the prow of the canoe lightly touched the Cambridge shore, "shall not our intention be soon published the second time?"

Penelope hesitated for a moment, with her paddle still resting among the sedges which grew by the shore, and gazed thoughtfully into the water.

"And must our intention be published yet a second time? I had thought that once were enough."

"A second time, Penelope, and even a third time, according to the order of the General Court."[22]

"Do as thou wilt, Ezekiel," said Penelope, quietly. The young man stepped from the canoe, trampling down a clump of sedge, and extènded his hand to the girl. Penelope slowly arose, paused a moment as she adjusted her kerchief, which had slipped from her shoulder with the exertion of handling the paddle, drew her long gloves smoothly upward, until they met the sleeves of her russet gown, and took the outstretched hand. The canoe lurched slightly as he stepped over the gunwale, and with a little cry of alarm she sprang forward. She alighted upon the clump of sedge which Ezekiel's foot had trampled. It quivered beneath her weight, and again she gave a little cry of alarm. Her leap had been so sudden that Ezekiel was, for an instant, disconcerted; but seizing her about the waist, he swung her lightly upon the firm ground. The boat, meanwhile, receiving impetus from Penelope's foot as she sprang, was drifting from the shore. Ezekiel, without waiting to remove his shoes and stockings, stepped into the water, drew it to the bank, and secured it to its moorings, while Penelope looked her protest.

"Thou shouldst not have done so!" she exclaimed.

"But thy canoe! It would have gone down the river to the bay and out to sea."

"Dost thou not see that the tide is setting inward? The canoe would have returned to us."

"Alas, I am very dull! But I pray heaven that for us the tide may ever be setting inward."

"Thou art surely gloomy to-day; but wherefore?"

"I cannot tell, Penelope. Truly I should not be gloomy. Master Bellingham hath won the election, for which result we have long hoped. This alone should make me gay, had I not the great added happiness which thou hast granted; yet it did strike me as an ill omen that thy foot should slip, and that thou shouldst wellnigh fall, even as the words which gave me happiness fell from thy lips."

"But thou wert near to aid me, Ezekiel," urged Penelope. "I have little faith in signs and omens. But grant that this were an unlucky slip, thou didst take me in thy arms and bear me safe to shore. Thus will all evil be averted from us."

"God grant that it may be so!" said Ezekiel, reverently. "Upon the next Lord's day, then," he added, cheerfully, "the intention shall be published. I will speak with thy brother, Herbert, that it be also published in Cambridge, — unless," he added, " thou wilt hold speech with him concerning the matter."

" Yes, Ezekiel. Thou art burdened with many cares. I myself will speak with Brother Herbert."

" It is well, then. And now, dear Penelope, farewell for a time."

He seized the girl's hand and raised it to his lips. He held it for a moment, and then, drawing her closer to his side, he kissed her cheek. Penelope smiled, but said nothing. The young man moved away, but at a few paces he turned and waved his hand. The girl smiled again, and waved her hand in response.

" See that thou dry thy shoes well, Ezekiel," she called cheerfully.

Another wave of the hand was his response, and he disappeared from view in the direction of the ferry. It was with a strangely mingled feeling that he made his way back to the town and to the mansion of Governor Bellingham. The General Court was still in session; but he knew that his presence was not required, and he had little heart to enter the meeting-house and listen to the proceedings. Nor could he, as he entered the door of the mansion and ascended the stairs, define the feeling by which he was oppressed. The servant in blue and silver livery looked at him, as he passed through the hall, as if to learn whether he desired any service, and partly as if to conjecture the cause of the young man's apparent abstraction. Ezekiel passed the man without notice and ascended the stairs to the first landing. There he paused, and resting his hand upon the carved and twisted balustrade, addressed himself to the servant below : —

"Thy pardon, Malchus. I should not leave thee ignorant of our master's exaltation. Henceforth we serve the worshipful Governor

Bellingham, so made this day by the votes of people of the Colony."

" Heaven be praised ! " responded the man, with fervor. " May he rule righteously !" .

"Amen!" returned Ezekiel.

The man departed to take the news to the household. Ezekiel made his way to the library, closed the door, and threw himself into a great arm-chair before the fireplace. It was the same chair, he noticed, in which Penelope had sat upon the occasion of her first visit to the mansion. Then a cheerful fire had blazed and crackled on the hearth; but now the fireplace was a black, cheerless cavern, for it was early summer.

" We should have some asparagus branches in the fireplace, to enliven it," he thought, vacantly; and then he remembered that the feathery branches of the asparagus had not yet appeared. He sat for a time gazing into the fireplace, his hands clasping the carved arms of the great chair. They were carved

in effigy of dragons' heads, and he absently
felt the long polished tusks with his fingers,
and wondered who had been the cunning
workman across the sea who had fashioned
them. Once he glanced downward and looked
for a moment at the great claw-feet, and
again he wondered who had carved them and
what manner of man he was. Then he arose
and walked the floor as in deep thought, his
hands clasped behind him; yet his thoughts
wandered. He went to the window and gazed
out upon the low green mounds in the burying-
ground across the way,[23] and his fingers idly
drummed upon the pane. Again he turned
away and walked about the room, gazing
absently at its furnishings. He paused a
moment before the portrait of the late Madam
Bellingham, and wondered if she, were she
living, would be more or less kind toward
him in his suit for Penelope's hand. Then
again he threw himself into the great arm-chair,
and gazed again into the empty fireplace.

He noticed that the great brass andirons were not so brightly polished as when a winter fire blazed upon the hearth, and he made a mental memorandum to request Malchus to call the attention of the housekeeper to the neglect. Thus idly his thoughts wandered upon trivial matters, until at length he roused himself and began to wonder at his own indifference to the momentous events of the day. He did not realize that this condition of mind was but the reaction which comes after a long-continued nervous tension. The labor and anxiety which had continued through many weeks and months was ended in victory; yet, as he had expressed himself to Penelope, victory had not brought with it that satisfaction for which he had hoped and which he had fully expected. Why was this? He tried to explain it to himself by the fact that the governor's majority had been much smaller than he had anticipated. He had looked for a more earnest expression of the people's will.

He tried to explain it, too, by the whisperings of discontent which he had heard in the market-place, and by the antagonism which had so early been developed between the new governor and the General Court. Yet none of these explanations sufficed to account for his lack of satisfaction and for his feeling of depression. He roused from his reverie at the ringing of the supper bell and went down absently. He ate sparingly and soon returned to the library, where he awaited the governor.

It was late when Ezekiel heard the heavy tread ascending the stairs, and he hastened to open the door for the governor. The candles had long been lighted, and the room presented a cheerful appearance as the chief magistrate entered. He at once removed his ruby-hilted sword and laid it upon the table, just where it lay when Penelope had made her first visit to the mansion. Perhaps the circumstance served, through .a process of association, to recall to the governor's mind this visit; for he exclaimed, as he threw himself into the great arm-chair : —

"I would, Ezekiel, that Mistress Penelope were here with thee, to welcome me with congratulations. But it will not be long; that thou must promise me."

"I promise that gladly, your worship."

"So we have succeeded, we have succeeded," said the governor, gleefully, yet with a slight restraint of manner.

"At last, yes," responded the secretary. "The Lord be praised!"

"Amen!" responded Governor Bellingham, but with some lack of fervor. Then both sat for some moments in silence. At length the governor spoke.

"I have no wish to detain thee later, Ezekiel, for thou must be weary. I myself shall be busy with my thoughts yet a little while."

"But thou art still fasting, good sir, and

the hour is late. Wilt thou not that I bid Malchus serve thee here?"

"Yea, Ezekiel, I had forgot the needs of the body. Yet I cannot sleep at once. Let Malchus serve me here."

Ezekiel gave the necessary order, as he left the room, bidding a good-night to the governor. Then he retired to his room and to bed. But the gray dawn was stealing into the eastern sky before his eyelids closed in slumber.

Chapter VIII.

THE young man lost no time in availing himself of the permission granted by Penelope, and the second and the third publication of the bans were made in rapid succession. The summer passed quickly, though to the impatient Ezekiel the weeks moved with leaden wings. It had been determined that the nuptials should take place in midwinter, and the young girl's wheel and loom were busy, as day by day the snow-white linen grew beneath her hand. For a time the gossips were busy in discussing the future of the young people. But as both were favorites, the speech of the gossips was kind, and only good wishes

fell from their lips. The young men envied
Ezekiel the rare good fortune which promised
him so lovely a woman for his wife. The
young women agreed that the Colony contained none more gallant and more pious than
Ezekiel, and that Penelope had done excellently
in her choice. Some of her nearest friends
begged her acceptance of pieces of linen from
their own looms, while others sent great skeins
of unbleached woollen yarn made upon their
own wheels, from wool grown in the sheep
pasture upon the Neck.

Thus the summer passed, and autumn came.
Governor Bellingham walked in his garden and
looked with pride upon the ripening clusters
of grapes upon the vine which he had planted
a year or two before, and which this year
had just begun to yield its fruit. A few late
autumn flowers lighted up the borders of the
paths with flashes of scarlet and of gold, and
the dry leaves rustled upon the ground. Upon
the trees a few clusters of leaves yet remained ;

but every passing breeze filled the air with tints of crimson, of brown, or of gold.

The governor's eyes lighted with pleasure as he saw a slender figure approaching slowly along the grass-fringed street, and he drew near the paling lest she should pass without his greeting.

" I salute thee, fair mistress," said the governor, gallantly, as Penelope drew near. The girl started with a sudden blush as she heard the words, and for the first time noticed the speaker. If the whole truth must be told, Penelope, whose way, quite by accident indeed, had fallen past the governor's mansion, was more intently watching the door than the garden, with the thought, no doubt, that perhaps Ezekiel might at that moment chance to come forth. The governor's salutation recalled her from a pleasant reverie. But she soon rallied from her embarrassment and dropped a modest courtesy to the governor, though the blush still mantled her cheek. She paused beside the paling. The governor lifted the great wooden latch which secured the gate, and swung it open.

"Wilt thou let me show thee my vine, Mistress Pelham?" he asked. "It hath but just borne its first fruitage. I was feasting my eyes upon it when I beheld thee drawing near."

"Yea, sir, it would please me well to see it," responded the girl. They walked side by side through the garden to the wall, against which hung the great purpling clusters, half hidden beneath the leaves. Governor Bellingham lifted them tenderly, one after another, almost lovingly, talking meanwhile to the pretty maid beside him. Both appeared distraught, and it was plain that she heard nothing. Suddenly he turned to the girl and addressed her more earnestly : —

"Thou hast not yet seen the new furnishings of my mansion, which arrived by the last ship."

"Nay, I had not so much as been acquainted with the knowledge of their arrival,". answered Penelope. "I do remember that Ezekiel did say, some months now agone, that thou hadst bade workmen in England send such hither. I remember it was on the day that thou wert chosen to be the governor that he told me. And have they so soon arrived?"

"Yea, they are within. Two days have passed since the good ship arrived which brought them."

"And it is full three days since Ezekiel sought me. He will come to-night, mayhap." And the blush deepened upon the soft cheek.

"Three days since he sought thee! In troth, Master Ezekiel is a laggard. So fair a mistress, and he three days absent!"

"Ezekiel hath ever told me," said the girl, with a little spirit, "that he seeketh his master's weal before his own pleasure."

"True, indeed, he is a faithful lad. Mayhap I myself am at the fault that he hath seemed

the laggard. Even now he hath gone, at my
bidding, to convey my message to good Master
Winthrop, at his island in the bay, whither he
hath gone to gather his fair pippins. But wilt
thou not enter, and with thine own eyes behold
what the good ship hath brought?"

They entered by the arched doorway leading
from the garden, the governor holding aside
the heavy crimson curtain for the young girl
to pass. The furnishings were, indeed, as
Ezekiel had said, fit for a governor's bride.
A heavy, richly carved bedstead of oak, with
lofty posts hung with tapestry, massive chairs
of like material, a chiffonnier, a table beauti-
fully inlaid, rich and costly hangings at the
windows, — these were some of the things upon
which the girl's eyes feasted, with a woman's
delight in fine adornings. The governor
watched her intently as she went from one
room to another with exclamations of delight.
At length they entered the library, and Penelope seated herself in the great arm-chair.

"Art thou well pleased, Mistress Pelham?" asked the governor.

"Indeed, sir, none could fail to see great beauty in what thou hast shown me."

"Since thou art pleased, the speech of others may not move me," said the governor.

"I, sir?" said Penelope, questioningly; and again her cheeks were crimson.

"Yea, Penelope; for thee I have bought these things and brought them hither."

The governor stepped before the girl and gazed steadily into her eyes. She could not understand his earnest gaze, and it disconcerted her.

"I remember me, sir," she said at length, "that Ezekiel said, as we talked together upon the day of the election, that thou hadst desired that we should take up our abode beneath thy roof; but I could scarcely believe such fortune to be ours, and had dismissed the thought."

8

"Ah, yes! Ezekiel did tell thee!" exclaimed the governor, as if disconcerted. He quickly crossed the room, and stood for a moment looking from the window. At the instant Kidby, the fisherman, passed, carrying in his hand a large cod. He glanced upward as he went, and saw the governor standing by the window; but the magistrate bestowed no cordial glance upon the humble fisherman, and he said to himself: —

"How now, Master Richard Bellingham, here is a fine cod, an thou wilt buy it, as thou didst at the spring-gate. I trow not! And did I not say so to my fellows, betimes? Even now, I'll warrant me, he plotteth against the people's rights. A wily man is Richard Bellingham." And the fisherman passed on, carrying his cod and muttering to himself.

Penelope was puzzled at the strange behavior of the governor. A moment later he whirled quickly away from the window and again approached the girl.

"Ah, yes, Ezekiel!" he repeated. "I had forgotten for the moment. And dost thou love him so much?"

"Love him, sir! But I have long since given to him my promise."

"Thy promise, — yes. But dost thou love him greatly?" pursued the governor.

The young girl attempted to reply; then her face grew crimson and she covered it with her hands.

"Let me not vex thee, Penelope," he said gently. "I had thought, mayhap —"

The girl looked up wonderingly, and the governor went on hastily: —

"I scarce know how to speak the words to utter all my thoughts. But hast thou done well? Cannot thy beauty and thy grace find place more meet for thee?"

The sweet face paled suddenly.

"Thou knowest naught of evil of Ezekiel, sir?"

"Of evil? Nay, fair mistress; Ezekiel is all that he doth seem to be. But yet —"

Penelope's face whitened, and she gazed
into the governor's eyes with a frightened look.

"Nay," said the governor again; "thou
shouldst have no fear. I had but thought,
Penelope, that 't were, better to rule than to
serve."

The white, fixed look still remained upon
the young girl's face, and she made no answer. The governor went on quietly, but
hesitatingly : ---

"Penelope, thou wilt soon be a bride.
But hast thou no choice? Wouldst thou wed
the servant, the rather — the rather than the
master?"   .

The blood returned to the girl's face with
a sudden rush, and her heart gave a bound
and then seemed to stop its beating. Still she
made no answer.

"Mistress Pelham," pursued the governor,
"I must say to thee more. I would not wrong
thee, nor yet Ezekiel. But thou and he well
know that he hath naught save my bounty.

As his wife thou wouldst be but a dependent. But as mine — as mine — Penelope — "

Penelope suddenly started to her feet, over-turning as she did so the great arm-chair, which fell with a sudden crash upon the floor. She stood an instant, rigid and cold, without motion. Then she rushed toward the broad window, and casting herself upon the crimson cushion which filled the alcove, buried her face in its folds. The governor quickly followed the girl, and drew about her the rich, heavy drapery of the window.

" It is only the great chair accidentally overturned," he explained to Malchus, who, at that moment, alarmed at the noise, knocked at the door. " Thou mayst replace it." The governor stood calmly upon the rug before the fireplace, and his countenance gave no token of an unusual mental disturbance. The man raised the chair to its feet, and, bowing, withdrew.

The door had scarcely closed when from the

crimson folds of the curtain came a low wail.
Then came a torrent of sobs, which shook the
slight form of the girl like a reed in a tempest.
Governor Bellingham remained in his position
upon the rug, unmoved amid this tumult, and
wearing an unchanging countenance. At last,
as the sobs grew gradually less, he approached
the window and quietly drew aside the curtain.
He stood for a moment looking down upon the
girl, her form still shaken with the violence of
her emotions. He laid his hand lightly upon her
head, and softly stroked the fair hair. Through
the broad window fell upon it a bright shaft of
sunlight, which for a time lighted it as with a
golden aureole ; but as the governor gazed,
marvelling at the wonderful beauty, a cloud
shut in the sunlight, and the aureole faded
away and came not again.

"Penelope, Penelope !"

Slowly the golden head was raised from the
crimson cushion, and the tear-stained cheeks
were turned toward the governor.

"Penelope," he said, "I would not distress thee, neither, as I have said, would I wrong thee nor Ezekiel. But, plainly, Penelope, I would have thee to wife. My deep affection must be my excuse and plead my cause. I am not versed in the arts of the suitor. I am a lonely man. Thy smile and thy voice, were they for me and for me alone, would brighten this lonely house, as could naught else. Wilt thou not be the governor's wife, Penelope?"

"Indeed, indeed, sir, I cannot answer thee now," — and she cast her glance upon the floor.

"Nay, Penelope, I do not demand thy answer now. Wait thee, but think. Think what the day will bring to thee that sees thee, not the secretary's wife, but the governor's. Then thou shalt be a leader, and not a follower. All mine shall be thine. Thou shalt ask nothing that shall not be given. Thou shalt be the mistress of all."

The governor took her hand for an instant; but she withdrew it and clasped her hands before her face. Then she murmured as if to herself: —

"Poor, poor Ezekiel!"

Poor Ezekiel, indeed! O crafty alchemist! The rod of gold plunged in the flask of love hath already turned its waters to pity!

The governor did not understand that he had already won. He looked slightly disconcerted as the words fell from the girl's lips. Then he seized one of the long braids of yellow hair that fell from her shoulders.

"Penelope, wilt thou not give me this?" he asked, loosening the ribbon which bound the tress. She started suddenly and the rich color again deepened in her cheeks.

"Nay, nay," she said quickly, "not that, not that! This one, if thou wilt, but not that."

"And why not the other, Penelope?" persisted Governor Bellingham.

"Because — because," — and the voice dropped low and plaintive,—"because Ezekiel did give it to me."

"Ezekiel, Ezekiel!" muttered the governor, stalking hastily across the room and as hastily returning.

"Indeed, indeed, I must hence, away," said the girl; "too long already have I lingered."

"Nay, let me still detain thee," urged the governor.

"Nay, nay, it must not be. The day waneth and I must go. And then, too, —"

"And then?"

"He may return, and I cannot, I cannot see him now, and here. I pray thee, let me go."

"Ah!" said the governor, "mayhap it may be well. But thou wilt give good thought to my discourse."

PENELOPE returned to her home, scarcely knowing which way she went. Her mind was torn with divers emotions. At one moment a feeling of indignation possessed her that the governor should thus rudely shatter her dream of bliss. She was indignant both for herself and for Ezekiel, and she firmly resolved that, when she and Ezekiel should be married, she would tell him of the governor's treachery, and he would leave his worship's service. They would go away together and live in a little cottage. They could live, she knew, without the governor's patronage. Ezekiel's

arms were strong, — and was she not deft with
her spinning-wheel?

Then would come up a vision of the beautiful rooms and costly furnishings that the
governor had shown her, and she would hear
his words : "All mine shall be thine. Thou
shalt ask for nothing that shall not be given.
Thou shalt be the mistress of all." Then
came the thought, "How much better this
than the cottage and, it may be, want!"
The governor's wife ! Wealth, social position,
all that woman could wish, might be hers,
would she but reach forth her hand and take it.
The fruit was beautiful to the eye ; would it
not be delicious to the taste? The thought
was fascinating ; and although she frequently
repelled it, as often would it return to her.

Then would come a rush of tears unbidden,
and a feeling of tenderness stole upon her, as
she thought of Ezekiel's last look and words.
She lived over again the scene in the forest,
when he knelt before her and gathered up

the fresh blossoms scattered at her feet. She
saw him with his hands outstretched toward
her, his hat upon the still moist ground. She
heard again, in memory, the words of love
which he spoke to her, and she felt again the
swelling wave of happiness as it arose in her
soul. Then she thought of Ezekiel's long and
patient waiting, of his earnest labors for his
master's advancement, of his goodness and of
his kindness towards her, of his tenderness,
of a thousand little attentions which he had
shown her, and which she at the time had
accepted but as matters of course.

Then her thoughts drifted onward to her
first visit to the governor's mansion. She recalled his politeness, his gallantry, so remark
able in the Puritan, so natural to a cavalier.
She thought of the kindness which he had
always shown her since that day, — a kindness
rendered not in a spirit of condescension, but
betokening a genuine friendly feeling toward
her and interest in her and her fortunes.

"Can it be," she asked herself, "that his worship, the governor, hath had this thing in mind from the very first? Can it be that he hath coveted me for himself, the while that he hath urged that Ezekiel and I be made one flesh? Nay, this cannot be! Had such been his intent from the first, he would not have thus hazarded his own interests. It must have been a thought born only of the moment, a sudden freak of mind or gust of passion, that even now he hath repented him of. He will not seek me to urge his suit. When sleep hath dispelled the vapors of the brain, and the world looketh clear again to his eyes, he will think no more of me. Mayhap to-morrow he will not so much as remember that he hath so given speech to me. Pray God he may not! I cannot, I cannot give Ezekiel up and never be his wife, even to be the wife of the governor. I will say naught of this to any one, — naught to my brother Herbert, nor yet to his wife, — naught to Ezekiel."

Then once more came the temptation, and
Penelope bowed herself before it as the reed
bows itself before the raging wind. Deep,
strong, and overwhelming it came upon her.
She saw herself honored and courted as the
first lady of the Colony, the leader in its
social life. She saw herself the envy of all
the young girls with whom she was familiar.
She alone, out of them all, had drawn upon
herself a governor's eyes and won a governor's
heart. How honored was she above them all
by his preference! Yet she would bear herself meekly. All those who had been her
friends should be the friends of the governor's
wife. Her elevation should in no wise increase
her pride. She would still be gentle and
humble, and she would still wear her hair in
braids. But, no! Would this be befitting
her station? Must she not bear herself with
greater dignity, and put her hair up beneath
·her cap? She would be the patron of all
good works among the people. She would

care for the poor, and they would bless her.
She would encourage the newly founded school.
Perhaps some day the governor would be summoned to London, and she would go with
him and be presented to the king and queen.
Then her imagination took on wild flights of
fancy, and she saw herself honored at home
and fêted abroad. All roseate was the future
for her. Surely never before did Puritan
maiden dream such blissful and such ambitious dreams.

Then again she came to herself, and with
the consciousness came a great revulsion of
feeling and almost an agony of remorse.

"Oh, Ezekiel, Ezekiel!" she moaned aloud.
"How wicked am I, and how good and how
kind art thou! How have I wronged thee in
my thoughts,—wronged thee and myself also!
I love thee, and thee alone. I cannot give
thee up,— no, not for the governor and his fine
house and his gold."

Then she became conscious that she had

spoken aloud, and she glanced quickly about, lest she should have been overheard ; but she saw no one, and heard nothing save the sad cry of the whip-poor-will, which came to her through the fast-settling gloaming. The sound recalled her more fully to herself, and she quickened her footsteps.

"Naught of this will I tell to Brother Herbert, nor yet to his wife," she repeated to herself, assuringly. "Within my own bosom will I keep this secret, — for a time, at least," she added to herself, compromisingly, as she opened the door of her home and entered.

She passed quietly to her own room, and endeavored to remove the traces of her recent agitation. Then she went softly down the stairs and entered the "keeping room." Her efforts at composure were vain ; for it did not escape the eye of Mistress Pelham, the elder, that something unusual and of moment had occurred. The two women were alone, and the

elder quickly approached the younger and laid her hand upon her shoulder.

"Sister Penelope," she said, "what hath happened? Thou art disquieted."

Penelope turned away her head and dropped her gaze upon the floor.

"Nay, sister; it is nothing."

"Penelope," pursued the other, "I am to thee in thy mother's stead. I adjure thee, tell this thing to me, even as thou wouldst to her. Hath aught gone amiss with thee?"

"Nay, nay, sister; naught hath gone amiss with me, but — but — " and she burst into tears and threw herself upon the great settle in the chimney corner.

Mistress Pelham, now alarmed, seated herself by the moaning girl and passed her arm about the slender waist. In another moment she was sobbing out upon her sister's shoulder the whole dreadful story.

"But I will never, never marry him," she said vehemently, as she closed the recital.

9

"Will never marry whom? — Ezekiel?"

"Nay, the governor."

"Thou wilt not marry Governor Bellingham!" exclaimed the sister, in amazement.

"Nay, indeed, but thou wilt marry him, Penelope."

Penelope cast down her eyes, but shook her head.

"Poor Ezekiel! Oh! I cannot do it," she moaned.

"Ezekiel! yes, — I had forgotten Ezekiel for the time."

"Forgotten Ezekiel!" The girl looked up quickly, almost angrily.

"Forgive me, dear Penelope, but I was overwhelmed for the moment. I had forgotten that thou and he were published. I must talk with Herbert. He will find us a way out of this entanglement."

"Oh! I pray thee, Priscilla, do not hold speech with Herbert."

"And wherefore, child? Nay, but I must.

It is a matter of no small import, and one
that doth deeply concern the family weal. I
could not do my duty and withhold this thing
from him. Herbert must surely know that
Governor Bellingham doth seek thee to wife."

Penelope said no more, but again cast her
gaze upon the floor and wept softly.

" Come, Penelope," said Mistress Pelham
at length. " It is past candle-lighting; the
table is spread for supper, and thy brother
will soon be here. Bestir thyself and. light
the candles."

" 'T were better to eat by the firelight,"
said the girl, persuading herself that by such
a light her agitation would not be so readily
betrayed.

" Nay, nay; Herbert would call for candles. 'T is better so." Then, as if divining
the girl's motive, she added kindly, " Have
thou no fear, Penelope ; neither desire thou
to conceal this thing. It concerneth us all.
We will advise thee to thy good."

It was long after Penelope had retired to
rest that night before sleep came upon her.
But when, at last, nature demanded a respite
and her long lashes swept the pillow, in her
dreams she stood before a lofty mirror. It
was greater than any that she had ever seen
before. In it she saw her own reflected form,
clad in cloth of gold. Around her floated a
wonderful veil of the rarest lace, and she
held in her hands a great cluster of blood-
red roses. She lifted them to her face, but
as she inhaled their fragrance, lo! they were
not roses, but a cluster of fresh mayflowers.
As she gazed upon them, mystified at this
sudden and strange transformation, she saw
that they were fading, and presently they
withered away within her hand. She flung
from her the faded flowers, but they had
scarcely left her grasp when they fell and
were scattered at her feet. Then a vision of
a young man crossed the polished plate and
gathered up the scattered flowers. Then he

gazed upward into her face, and as she glanced down upon him, behold, it was not a fresh, young face which looked into hers. It was old and faded and wrinkled, and framed about with locks like hoarfrost. The lips moved, but uttered no sound. "Who can this be?" she thought; and then a look of tenderness and of grief crossed the aged face, and she thought of the encounter in the forest of Rocksbury. Then, as the face began to take on a familiar look, the form receded and disappeared in the distance. She gazed after it with a longing which she could not define. Then, in the background, as the form faded, she saw, and as she looked she shuddered, a row of new-made graves, and the mayflowers which she had flung from her were growing and blooming upon them. Then a voice seemed to recall her, and a sudden light flashed across the mirror, and the sound of music came softly dropping

down. And a strong voice said to her,
"Come, Penelope."

She awoke, and her heart was beating
wildly, half in fear and half in gladness. All
was dark, and no sound broke the stillness,
save the solemn ticking of the tall clock upon
the stairs. She lay for a moment trying to
recall what had happened. Slowly the clock
struck three, and with the sound came a rush
of memory. She remembered it all. She
turned upon her couch and, burying her face
in the pillow, cried softly. Then like a flash
came upon her the remembrance of her
dream. She saw again before her the sad,
aged face, with the whitened locks and the
deep blue eyes, which she knew so well.
Then, with a gasp and a shudder, she saw
again the row of new-made mounds and
the arbutus nestling amid the grass. "What
could it mean?" she thought, and then again,
this time with terror, she heard the words,

which seemed to her a command, "Come,
Penelope." All was so real that she could
not repress a cry of fear, which rang through
the quiet house.

Priscilla was at the girl's bedside in an
instant, her arms about her and her warm
lips pressed to the cold cheek.

"What is it, dear Penelope?" she asked.

"Is it thou, dear Priscilla? Ah, me! I am
so distraught."

"I will light a candle; so shall we drive
away the demons that distress thee."

"I pray thee, Priscilla, wilt thou not lie
with me until the morning?" begged Penelope.

"Yea, surely, if so I might drive fear from
thy heart," answered Mistress Pelham. She
took the tinder-box from its place upon the
shelf, struck a light, and lighted a candle.
Placing it upon a small stand in one corner,
she adjusted a screen before it. Then she
lay down beside the girl, and drew the throb

bing head upon her shoulder. For a while neither spoke. Then Penelope whispered, —

"Hast thou held speech with Herbert, Sister Priscilla?"

"Yea, Penelope. But fear not, and possess thy soul in peace. I pray thee go to sleep."

Chapter X.

GOVERNOR BELLINGHAM stood at the window, half concealed by the heavy crimson curtain, and watched the young girl as she walked somewhat hurriedly down the street. He did not wish to seem to be watching her; and so, when he saw Kidby returning and without his cod, he drew the curtain more closely about him, and shrank back slightly from the window.

"An impudent fellow, the fisherman Kidby," he muttered. "I dealt kindly with him, and what did he in return? If all be true that goeth about the town, this fellow did much to foment discontent among the people. I' faith," said the governor to himself as he strode angrily to his chair before the great writing-table, "and I have some belief that but for him and his gabbling tongue Richard Bellingham would have been the governor by far more than six votes. But yet it served, it served."

He cast himself in the chair where he had sat in meditation upon the night when he first returned to his mansion, the governor of the colony.

"Yea, it served," he repeated to himself alone. "Richard Bellingham is not one to be foiled."

He sat long, wrapped in thought, and did not observe the shadows slowly filling the room. A tap upon the door aroused him, and Malchus entered with candles. He placed them upon the table and upon the tall mantel, and fixed others in the brass sconces on the wall.

"Ah, Malchus, I thank thee. I had not

observed the gathering of the gloaming. Hath Master Bolt yet returned?"

"Nay, sir."

"Say'st thou so? Can harm have come to him? He went hence while yet the sun was high, bearing a message to the worshipful Master Winthrop, whom forsooth he must seek at his island in the bay."

As he spoke the front door of the mansion was heard to close, and a step sounded upon the stairs.

"He hath returned. It is well," said the governor.

"The Lord is good," said Malchus. As he withdrew, Ezekiel entered.

"Ah, good Master Ezekiel," exclaimed the governor. "And thou hast returned. I had begun to fear me lest evil had befallen thee."

"Nay, good sir; the Lord is good, and hath kept me from harm."

"And thou didst find Master Winthrop at the island?"

"Yea, and did give to him thy message. He held speech with me at length concerning the matter thereof."

"Ay! We will talk together upon these things on the morrow. I am weary to-night. I rely upon thee, Ezekiel. Hast supped, my lad?"

"Nay, sir."

"Call Malchus, I pray thee, and we will sup together."

They sat almost in silence until the meal was nearly finished. At length the governor spoke.

"How goeth thy matters with fair Mistress Penelope?" he asked. "I had wellnigh forgot to tell thee that she hath been here while thou wert gone. I did regret deeply that thou wert not here, that thou might'st have shown to her the new furnishings; but to atone for her disappointment, I did my best, and myself became her courier."

"She hath been here?" queried Ezekiel. "And wherefore?"

"Nay, she came not of her own will. She but passed while I walked in the garden; and I, in duty bound, since she is pledged to thee, begged of her that she would come within. I shewed to her the grapes upon the vine; then the new furnishings, whereat she was pleased to say that they delighted her."

"Thou art very kind. I sorrow that I was not here to greet her."

"Thou lovest her greatly, Ezekiel?"

"Yea, sir. Were I to lose this great happiness that is promised me, my life would be as nothing."

"Ah, the ardor of youth!" said the governor. "And youth cometh but once. And thou art nearly ready to be contracted?" he continued, as they arose from the table.

"Yea, sir. In midwinter we shall be married," answered the secretary.

"Ah! That is well. A good wife is of the Lord, Ezekiel."

"I must, perforce, have told him of her coming," the governor said to himself when he was alone in his chamber. "He would have learned it from others. In midwinter! Art thou not over-sure of thy future, Master Ezekiel?"

In the morning the governor arose and looked from his window. As he turned his eyes toward his garden, two birds hovered about the pane, and sought to build their nest among the branches of the tree which overshadowed it. As he looked, a hawk swooped suddenly down, and seizing one of the birds, bore it away in his talons. The poor mate fluttered his wings in helpless protest, but he could do nothing, and he was left alone to wail out his sorrow upon the air.

With the morning had come to Governor Bellingham a resolution. He must have time to think, and he must be by himself. At all events he must be, for a time, apart from

Ezekiel. He would visit his farm at Winnisimmet. It was harvest time, and he always visited the farm at harvest time. Ezekiel would think nothing strange of this.

Strangely enough, Governor Bellingham had, within the past few hours, begun in a wonderful degree to regard Ezekiel as in some way a part of himself, and to imagine that he must govern his own acts largely by what he imagined Ezekiel would think of them. A strange bondage it was, and one to which Bellingham was unaccustomed. Yet he pondered long upon the subject, in his early waking hours, ere he could persuade himself that in the going to Winnisimmet Ezekiel could not possibly suspect a desire to be for the time rid of his presence. It seemed to him an unnatural thing to do, — or rather that Ezekiel would so regard it; but still, was it not harvest time, and was it not his invariable custom to visit his farm at that season of the year? For the first time in his life the governor felt like one who carries about his person the evidence of his crime, hidden from the sight of all, yet to his guilty mind plainly visible to the world. So does sin "make cowards of us all."

He announced his intention to Ezekiel at breakfast, and soon after set out by himself. It was one of those rich, warm days in the late autumn, when the air is full of a golden haze, and when the deep blue sky seems to hang lower over the earth than at midsummer. It was early for the governor to be abroad; too early indeed, for the town to be much astir. Yet now and then he met a shopkeeper, whom he greeted with a condescending nod, or else passed without notice.

At the outset he had thought to cross to Winnisimmet by the ferry; but when he had walked part of the way to the landing he suddenly bethought him that Thomas Marshall, the ferryman, lodged at the opposite side, and that it was too early yet for him to be abroad.

"I will, forsooth, row myself thither in my own boat," said the governor to himself. "Thus I may gain an hour of time, and it will be healthful as well."

Diverging a little from the path which he was following, he went to his own landing, and with some exertion pushed the boat into the water from where it lay upon the beach. He sat for a moment or two upon the thwart, looking about him. Once he fancied that he saw Ezekiel coming slowly down the street toward the landing, and he seized his oars with a sudden grasp, and with an impulse to escape; then he bethought him of the folly of this, and was ashamed of his trepidation. In a moment more he discovered it was not Ezekiel who approached, but Angola, — a negro well known about the town as a servant of Captain Robert Keayne.

Idly resting upon his oars, the governor

watched Angola as he approached the landing, cast off the painter of a boat and, a
moment later, pulled with strong, steady
strokes toward Noddle's Island. Then the
governor seized his oars again and turned his
boat's prow toward Winnisimmet. He was
deeply absorbed in his thoughts, and did not
observe that at every stroke the bow of the
boat plunged deeper and deeper into the
water. He did not perceive that aught was
amiss until he suddenly realized that the water
was about his ankles. Then, starting, he saw
that the boat, from lying long unused upon
the shore, had become started at the seams
and was already half filled with water, and
was rapidly settling. He at once perceived
that the entire submersion of the boat was
a matter of but a few moments.

A horror which only they can realize who
have passed through danger of death possessed
Governor Bellingham's soul. For an instant
he was speechless, and sat gazing with terror

upon the fast-advancing water; then, dropping his oars, he grasped the gunwale, and
sought to cry aloud for help. But his voice,
hoarse with fear, refused to obey his will, and
he could only gasp in sibilant whispers, "Lord,
save, or I perish!"

Slowly, slowly sank the boat, and with it
sank Governor Bellingham. Again he gazed
upward and about him. The day was fair.
Already the sun, an hour high, was casting a
flood of golden light across the water. Nature
was fair; yet Nature was slowly but surely
engulfing him who gazed. Again he sought
to cry for help, but his voice only came back
to him again in hoarse and startled whispers.
The next moment the boat lurched, and the
governor was thrown into the water. With a
long, piercing cry, he sank. The boat, now
filled, settled to the water's level, and the blue
waves of the Charles rippled as quietly as if
they had not closed above the head of the
Governor of the Colony.

A moment later the drowning man came to the surface, gasping for breath, and despairingly clutching the empty air. Was it the kind Providence which he had invoked that guided his hands to the almost submerged gunwale of his sunken boat? A sense of relief swept over him and unsealed his lips. He cried long and loud for help. He neither saw nor heard the boat that, propelled by the powerful strokes of two dusky arms, was rapidly coming to his rescue. He continued to shout for help until he felt a strong grasp upon his shoulder and heard rough but hearty words of cheer.

"Help me ! help me ! " gasped the governor.

"Ay, Marster Bellingham ; Angola will save thee, marster."

With a strong hand Angola drew the governor into his boat. Taking his own cloak, which lay across a thwart, he wrapped it about the dripping form ; then, resuming his oars, he turned the boat's prow toward the town.

The governor crouched silently in the stern, and shivered as he wrapped the negro's cloak more closely about him. For a time he said nothing. Then, as the boat neared the shore, he spoke.

"Good Angola, thou hast saved my life. But for thee I should have gone hence, ere this moment. Thou shalt be rewarded, as surely as the day cometh. What wilt thou that I give to thee?"

"Nay, Marster Bellingham, I desire nothing," answered the negro; "I am glad."

"But," insisted the governor, "I must give thee something for a remembrance. Wouldst not like a piece of ground?"

The negro looked into his face for a moment, and then said, —

"Angola would like a garden."

"It shall be so. Thou shalt have my piece of ground, near the Neck, on the highway which leads to Rocksbury; and I will have a fence put about it for thee." [24]

GOVERNOR BELLINGHAM kept his room closely for three days after his mishap, and for the most of that time his bed. On the fourth day he ventured out, and was received on all sides with congratulations upon his narrow escape from death. Those who agreed with him in matters of public concern and those who were his most bitter opponents in his candidacy for gubernatorial honors were equally eager to extend their expressions of gladness. Even Kidby, the fisherman, doffed his hat as the great man approached, and smiled in unison with the general joy.

During the time of his confinement to his chamber the governor had had time for profound thought. Ezekiel waited upon him daily for directions, but the same feeling which prompted him to go to Winnisimmet also induced him to refrain so far as was possible from calling upon his young secretary during his illness. It happened, therefore, that Ezekiel saw but little of the governor during these days; yet he dared not absent himself from the house for any considerable space of time, lest his presence should be demanded in the governor's chamber. He had welcomed his master's departure for Winnisimmet, for the occasion would be also his own opportunity to visit Cambridge; but now he must forego this pleasure, for some days at least. It was with some impatience, therefore, that he awaited the governor's convalescence.

Governor Bellingham had anticipated this impatience. He well knew Ezekiel's faithfulness, and was confident that he would not

leave the premises for a space of time suffi-
cient for a visit at Herbert Pelham's house.
Of this he felt certain. But he knew well
that, upon his own restoration to health, Ezekiel's first impulse would be to seek Penelope.
He remained in his room a full day longer
than his health demanded, that he might solve
this perplexing problem.

Suddenly all became clear to him. He
would affect impatience to learn how matters
were thriving at his farm at Winnisimmet,
which his mishap had prevented him from
visiting. He would despatch Ezekiel thither
on the morrow. The secretary having safely
gone, he himself would go to Cambridge and
urge his suit, if possible, to success.

Ezekiel felt a pang of disappointment that
his projected visit must be still longer delayed ;
but he went forth willingly, early the next
morning, at his master's bidding.

"I shall be about ere thou dost return,
Ezekiel," said the governor at parting. "I

am better to-day. To-night we will sup together."

The governor arose when Ezekiel had left the chamber; but he waited until the young man had left the house before he made the fact known to the household. When from his chamber window he saw his secretary walk briskly away, he summoned Malchus, and directed that breakfast be served. This over, he arrayed himself with unusual care. "For," he thought, "I shall meet many by the way who will inquire of my health." Then he sallied forth, before the gaze of men, mounted his bay horse,[25] and turned his face toward Cambridge.

It was with a curious feeling that the governor, with his horse's bridle across his arm, sounded the great brass knocker upon the door of the house of Herbert Pelham. Had he stopped to analyze this feeling, it would, no doubt, have proved to be a mingling of shame born of duplicity, of youthful trepidation, and of assurance resultant upon a possession of authority; but he gave himself no time for thought, and with some effort, it is true, forced the last-named attribute to the forefront.

"Is good Master Pelham within?" he inquired of the maid who answered his knock.

"Yea, good sir; he is within. Wilt enter?" replied the girl, throwing wide the door, for she recognized the governor.

Penelope, who had from her window seen the approach of the governor, fled instantly, as she heard his knock, to the innermost room of the house. Closing the door, she threw herself upon the floor and pressed her cheek hard against the boards, covering her face with her hands. Every sense was alert and listening. For a long time she lay thus, motionless, intent upon the slightest sound, yet dreading to hear her name. It seemed to her that days and nights passed as thus she lay. At last her acute senses discerned a light footfall in a distant room. A door opened and closed softly. It was the door of her chamber, and Priscilla was seeking her.

Penelope made no sign, but still lay, her cheek pressed hard against the floor and her senses strained to the utmost. The footstep drew nearer, and the door of the chamber where she lay was softly opened.

"Penelope, child! Art thou here? I have sought thee everywhere. Come, arise! Governor Bellingham would see thee."

Penelope's only answer was to turn her face slightly and look upon her sister-in-law as she stood in the doorway.

"What aileth thee, child?" asked the elder, a trifle impatiently. "Thou art not ill? Arouse thee and dress thyself, and come down at once."

Penelope raised herself upon one hand to a half-reclining position, and stared at Priscilla with set eyes and white face. The matron, alarmed, seized the girl's shoulder and shook it slightly.

"Arouse thee, Penelope! Look not at me with that stony stare. Let me help thee to thy chamber."

The girl struggled to her feet, and suffered herself to be led to her own room. In the same passive manner she submitted to be dressed in her bravest attire, and at last to be led down to the best room. At the door she paused and shrank backward.

"I cannot, Priscilla; indeed I cannot," she said piteously.

"Thou canst, Penelope! Thou must come in and greet his worship, for he doth call for thee. Come thou with me."

At the word, the matron threw open the door, and drew the pale and shrinking girl within. Governor Bellingham arose, advanced, and took her hand.

"Penelope!" he said.

The girl for an instant lifted her eyes from the floor and rested them upon the face of the governor. Then again the long golden lashes swept the cheek, and her gaze fell before his.

"Nay, I pray thee," remonstrated the governor, as those present rose to withdraw, at a swift signal from Priscilla, "good Master Pelham, wilt thou not tarry, thou and thy wife, until this business shall be finished?"

"If it be thy wish, we will remain," answered Herbert Pelham.

"So be it," responded the governor. "And now, Penelope," he resumed, drawing the still shrinking girl to a chair beside him, "hast thou given good heed to my discourse to thee some days agone?"

"Yea," answered Penelope, in a tone so low that it seemed but a sigh.

"And so, forsooth, have I," said the governor.

Penelope caught her breath quickly, and flashed a glance at the governor's impassive face.

"I also have given it good heed," he went

on, with great deliberation : " and in it I have seen naught to regret. For three days now past, a prisoner in my chamber, I have given thought to little else. I told thee before, Penelope, and I tell thee now, I seek thee to wife."

Still the girl's eyes were bent downward, but a slight flush tinged the pallor of her cheek.

"May I ask thee for an answer to my suit, Penelope?" he urged. "Wilt thou be the wife of Governor Bellingham?"

Penelope raised her eyes to the governor's face, and met his gaze with a look clear and firm, as she said very softly, —

"Yea, if the Lord so will."

Then, as the words fell from her lips, she started and clasped her hands upon her breast, as if stung to the soul with a sudden remembrance. A silence fell upon the group for a moment, which was broken by Herbert.

"What may prove to thee a strong barrier, may it please the governor," he said, "has but

this moment occurred to me, — the banns!
Have they not been published in the meeting-
houses, both here and in Boston? Will the
godly ministers or the magistrates unite thee
and her?"

The governor started, and a flush arose to
his face.

"The magistrates!" he exclaimed. "Is not
the governor of his Majesty's Colony of Massachusetts Bay a magistrate who outranks them
all? Who shall say to Governor Bellingham,
'Do ye so'? Have I not in me all authority
which in another lieth?"

"It is even so," said Herbert, bowing low.

The flush mounted higher in the governor's
face as he paused, and a deathlike silence pervaded the room. Then, seizing the hand of
Penelope, he led her to the centre of the room,
and standing there, with his arm about the
girl's waist, demanded, —

"Summon thy household, good Master
Pelham, and they shall see Governor Belling-

ham's power. Now, even this very hour, shall
Penelope Pelham be his bride."

A vivid flush rose to the girl's cheeks; but
she said nothing. Priscilla hastened to do the
governor's bidding; and a moment later the
people of the household timidly entered, and
stood in a throng about the door. The governor acknowledged their presence by a glance
and a slight inclination of the head.

"Penelope Pelham," he said, "wilt thou, in
the presence of these, take Richard Bellingham
to be thy lawful husband?"

"Yea, I will," softly answered Penelope.

"And I, Richard Bellingham, will take
thee, Penelope, to wife. And now I, the
governor of his Majesty's Colony of Massachusetts Bay, do pronounce and declare that
Richard Bellingham and Penelope Pelham
are man and wife together. The King shall
be my witness." [26]

A long-drawn sigh swelled through the
room; whence it came none could tell. At

the instant the throng parted, and a young man stood in the midst.

"Ezekiel!" gasped the bride.

A silence followed, broken at last by the governor.

"Thou art bewildered, Ezekiel, and wouldst know what this doth mean. Plainly I will tell thee, for I own thy right to know. Mistress Pelham did think to be thy wife; but I fear me that thou hast been a laggard, for another hath 'stepped down before thee.' Behold, Mistress Pelham hath wisely thought it better to be the wife the rather of the master than of the servant; and she is now no more Mistress Pelham, but Madame Bellingham, the governor's bride."

For an instant Ezekiel was stunned with the suddenness of the blow. Then, in a voice husky with grief, he spoke.

"Penelope, this is true?"

"Yea, it is true," she answered, without raising her eyes.

"And thou hast ceased to love me ! Thou hast forgotten thy promise made me in the forest ! Didst thou not promise me, or is it all a dream, Penelope, that thou wouldst be my wife?"

"Nay, Ezekiel," she answered softly; "it is no dream. I did promise thee, but if the Lord so willed."

"And thou hast broken thy promise, and the bans already published?"

"Nay, Ezekiel; but the Lord hath willed otherwise."

Ezekiel's pale face flushed to a deep crimson, and he burst forth, with all the passion of his soul, —

"Take heed, Madame Bellingham, that thou tempt not the name of the Lord. To thee this only, for thou hast been sore tempted; but thou hast broken a faithful heart. But to thee, to thee, sir, who art the defender of the peo-ple's rights, thou who hadst so much and I so little, couldst thou not have left to me but this?

Ah!" he gasped, clasping his hands over his eyes, "the morning-glories did wither as we clasped our hands above the paling! why saw I not the presage? And her foot did fail upon the sedge! How blind, how blind! But thou," and he turned fiercely upon the governor, "thou hast deeply, cruelly wronged me. Scarce three suns have set since thou didst commend my choice."

"But my deep affection," urged the wily governor.

"Thy deep affection, indeed! Is it deeper than mine, which hath its roots set in my soul? Nay, thou didst seek but a bauble, a toy, an ornament for thy mansion; and thou hast despoiled my life, and made it but dust and ashes. I go hence to a lifelong grief. Oh, the withered blossoms, the withered blossoms!"

Ezekiel gazed, with folded arms, upon the governor. Then his eyes, dull with grief, rested for a moment upon the bride. He raised his clenched hands above his head, as if to pronounce a curse. Then he let them fall again ; and casting upon Penelope a look of unutterable longing and reproach, he turned and burst from the door.

THE surprise of the people of the town was great when they saw Governor Bellingham returning across the Neck, with Penelope seated behind him upon a pillion. Still greater was their amazement when he drew rein at his own doorstep, assisted the girl to alight, and escorted her within, with ceremonious civility. It knew no bounds when it became known that the woman to whom he showed such marked courtesy was already his bride. From house to house, from shop to shop, the tidings flew; and great was the excitement and great the indignation of both magistrates and people.

"Is it not as I told thee?" demanded
Kidby, the fisherman, as he strode into Hudson's Ordinary, and threw a basket of fish
upon the floor. "Did I not say," he asked
fiercely, "that Richard Bellingham is no
friend of the people? But I own that I little
thought he would be so ungrateful."

"What hath happened, Kidby?" asked
Hudson, as a group gathered about the two.

"Hast not heard, gossip?" he asked wonderingly. "Am I truly the first to tell it?
Listen, then. But yesternight came knocking
at my door Ezekiel Bolt; and when I bade
him enter, he did seem greatly distraught,
and weak and faint withal. And when my
good wife had brought him meat, and he had
eaten, he saith : 'Prythee, wilt thou give me shelter, Kidby?' And I said : 'Surely, Master Bolt,
thou art welcome to the best that my house
can give to thee; but wherefore, I pray
thee?' Then he saith : 'Governor Bellingham
hath despoiled me. He did despatch me to

Winnisimmet, and when I had fairly gone, he hied him to Cambridge and tempted her who was to have been my wife, with his gold; and she hath become his bride and not mine.' And I said: 'Of a truth, she was promised to thee, and ye have already been published in the churches. How, then, under our righteous laws, can she be espoused to another?' And Ezekiel saith to me: 'Behold, Kidby, the governor hath himself taken the part of the magistrate, and hath pronounced himself and Mistress Pelham to be man and wife.' "

" Himself! " gasped the bystanders, in astonishment.

" It is so," said Kidby. "Governor Richard Bellingham hath transgressed our righteous laws, the which he hath sworn faithfully to execute."

" He should be presented by the great inquest," said Hudson, with indignation.

" Even so he should," agreed Waters Sinnott, who stood by. "It is not meet that the governor should break our laws, and we all be holden. He should be presented."

So said all who stood by.

"And what of Master Bolt?" inquired Hudson. "In troth, why came he not hither for shelter, and not trouble thy good wife?"

"Alack, good Master Hudson, and he hath not drawn his earnings of his worship, the governor, save as his need hath required. He had by him but a little" —

"And did Master Ezekiel Bolt bethink him that I would require aught of him? He should have known me better. Send him hither to me. He shall not want for shelter while William Hudson hath a roof above him. Full many a kindness hath he done to me."

"He is much distraught," said Kidby; "so that, forsooth, I feared me yesternight that he was beside himself. For he did toss upon his bed, and did mutter many times, as he slept : 'The withered blossoms, the withered blossoms !' "

" Aye, the poor lad," said another. " Dost know of what he spoke, Kidby? Mayhap it was not he who spoke, but some other through him. Canst see an omen? "

" Nay," answered Kidby; " he talked with her across the palings at Master Wilson's, upon the election day; and as they talked the blossoms of the morning-glory vines faded away. They but do so from day to day, as the sun waxeth. I see naught in it; but Ezekiel thinks it to have been a warning that he should have heeded."

" Mayhap it was, mayhap it was ! " muttered Sinnott.

Before the night fell, all in the town had heard the great news; but not a voice was heard to praise the governor's deed. The young men, with whom Ezekiel was a favorite, sympathized with him in his great grief. Many sought him at Hudson's Ordinary,

where he took up his abode, and warmly
expressed their indignation at the governor's
heartlessness. The older men and the magistrates, with whom Bellingham had never been
a favorite, openly avowed their disapproval.
The women, old and young, railed mercilessly
at the heartless conduct of Penelope, and
vowed that she could never more be to them
what she had been.

When the governor first appeared upon the
street, after his marriage, he was everywhere
greeted with cold and distant looks, with
glances of distrust and aversion. He was
surprised to find himself the object of a
crushing unpopularity. Former friends, he
realized, were now foes; and those who had
been already unfriendly were now more than
ever his enemies. He had thought that to
take a young wife, who would reopen his
mansion, that had been closed to the social
world since the death of his former wife,
would increase his hold upon the popular

heart, and render his triumph at the next election, now but a few months in the future, a foregone conclusion. He had reckoned upon the great popularity of the bright, young girl, Penelope, with the young freemen of the Colony; but he had sailed upon a false reckoning.

Meanwhile, as the storm of indignation swept over the town, a man broken in spirit sat listlessly in his room at Hudson's Ordinary. For hours together he would sit brooding over his great trouble, and gazing out of the window upon the water of the bay, wondering if it would ever be still. One day he was aroused from his reverie by Hudson, who announced a visitor below.

"What manner of man is he?" asked Ezekiel.

"Plainly to tell thee, it is Malchus, the serving-man of his worship, the governor," answered Hudson.

"What doth he desire?"

"Nay, I know not.   He hath not told me; neither did I ask of thy affairs.   Come thou down and ask of him, Ezekiel."

Ezekiel arose wearily, and walked heavily down the stairs.

"Thou didst call for me, Malchus?" he said to the man in waiting.

"Yea, Master Bolt.   His worship, the governor, did despatch me to find thee, and to give to thee this bag of gold," said Malchus, placing a bag of coin upon the table.

"Take thou back the governor's gold," said Ezekiel, "and say to him that Ezekiel Bolt hath no need of his charity."

"Nay, sir," entreated the man; "it is not charity, but thy due.   'Behold, these are his wages,' saith his worship."

"Nay, nay, I cannot touch his gold.   I want it not.   Take it back to Governor Bellingham, and say to him that I want it not.   'T would taint my touch."

"Nay, Ezekiel," urged Hudson; "it is thine own due. Why shouldst thou not take it?"

"'T is the price of my heart's blood," said Ezekiel, with a shudder. "Take thou it, Hudson, if thou wilt, and give it to them who order the town's occasions, that they may bury the poor withal. His worship, the governor himself, is one of these, and may tell how best to order it."

When Malchus had gone, Ezekiel turned toward the window again, and resumed his gaze upon the water.

"Come, then, my friend, this will never do," said William Hudson, laying his hand roughly, but kindly, upon his shoulder. "Thou must not brood, after this wise, over thy sorrow. There are still good fish in the sea. Let not thy life be despoiled by the vagaries of a fickle woman. Get thee up and go hence with Kidby. See, he waiteth for thee in his boat," continued Hudson, pointing from the window. "Go thou and cast thy line and forget thy grief."

"My grief .I cannot forget," answered Ezekiel; "but I will go with Kidby."

So it came about that the governor's secretary, forgetful of his former calling, went forth daily with his line, and became one with the fishermen of the port. His buoyancy of spirits was gone. He became a silent man, but not morose. He seldom spoke unless addressed, and then answered often with a sad smile. As, year after year, the spring-time came, he made it his custom to visit the forest of Rocksbury, and the earliest blossoms of the mayflower he was sure to find.

Still, the feeling of indignation toward the governor continued, and the opinion of the group of fishermen was echoed as the universal sentiment of the town. "He who breaketh our righteous laws," said they all, "must be presented, be he governor or magistrate or the humblest dweller among us." So it came about that as Governor Bellingham sat in his library there came a great knocking at his door, and a voice without cried : —

"Open thou, Richard Bellingham, in the law's name ! "

Then entered Nicholas Willys, the constable, bearing his white wand of office, and stood before the governor as he sat at his desk. Penelope, or, as we must now call her, Madame Bellingham, sat in the crimson cushioned alcove, half concealed by the heavy folds of the curtain.

"Know thou," said the constable, "that the great inquest hath presented thee, Richard Bellingham, for trial at our court, upon complaint that thou hast broken our righteous laws. Take thou heed, therefore, and answer to this summons."

As Willys spoke, he laid before the governor the warrant, and, without a bow, withdrew.

"An impudent fellow, forsooth," said Madame Bellingham, when the constable had gone. "Why made he not his obeisance to thee, the governor?"

"Nay," answered Bellingham, "Willys hath the right of it. He came in the law's name to wait upon Richard Bellingham, the freeman, and not the governor. He should not have made obeisance."

"But what wilt thou do," asked his wife, anxiously, "that the great inquest hath presented thee?"

"I am Richard Bellingham," answered the governor; "have thou no fear."

The gratification of the people of the Colony was great when it became known that an indictment had been found against the governor. It had been feared by some that, since he was himself a magistrate, this fact would serve to deliver him; but Puritan justice was stern and no respecter of persons. It was, therefore, with the greatest interest that the people awaited the coming of the day when the trial

of the governor should be held. When it at
last came, the room was crowded with the
freemen of the Colony. Here in the judge's
seat sat Winthrop the elder, and Sir Richard
Saltonstall, from among the magistrates. Hibbens and Tyng, the deputies, were here; and
here, too, were the men of the town, — Valentine Hill, the merchant, and Lysle, the
barber, and Davies, the gunsmith, and Tuesdale and Leverett, and behind them all the
broad shoulders and ruddy face of William
Hudson. Not a few women, too, elbowed
their way through the throng, and filled the
benches allotted to spectators. But among
them all none was more calm and self-
possessed, more indifferent to the gaze and
chatter of the crowd without, than was the
governor. The people shrank backward and
gave him room as he approached, and, as the
chief magistrate of the Colony, ascended the
bench and took his seat with Winthrop and
Saltonstall.

12

"Of a truth," said Sir Richard, in a low tone, to Winthrop, "Richard Bellingham surely will not himself sit while he is accused."

"It were not meet that he should do so," answered Winthrop.

"Have ye aught else to bring before us?" demanded Bellingham of the secretary, after he had heard and decided a few trifling causes. The people held their breath, and looked upon the secretary with anxious expectancy.

"We have naught else," answered the secretary, solemnly, "save a presentment against one Richard Bellingham, that he hath made a breach of the order of court."

"If ye have any causes that ye would bring against any person whatsoever, we will hear them," said the governor, while all marvelled at his boldness.

"But it is scarcely meet that a magistrate should sit in judgment upon his own cause," said the secretary. Winthrop and Sir Richard turned a glance upon each other at these

words; then looked upon Bellingham for his
answer.

"Nay, we know naught of these things,"
said Bellingham. "The magistrates must hear
what is brought before them. I will yield to
no one of my right and duty."

"And thou wilt not come down?" asked
the secretary.

"Nay," answered Bellingham, "I will not
come down except I am so commanded; and
who shall bid me?" he added in a low tone,
as if to himself.

"We must, perforce, put it off until another
time, then," said the secretary.

"If ye· have naught else to bring before
me, the court shall be adjourned," said the
governor.[27]

A silence deep and solemn fell upon all.
At last the secretary spoke : —

"We have naught else."

"Then let the officer adjourn the court,"
said the governor, and he swept from the

room, his robes of office rustling as he
went.

Still greater was the amazement of the
people when it became known throughout
the Colony that the governor had not only
broken the law, but had openly defied its
authority.

"We cannot have this man as our chief
magistrate," said one and another, in the
market-place and upon the street corners.
The fishermen, who were wont to gather for
gossip at Hudson's Ordinary, and among whom
Ezekiel was a hero, were loud in their denun-
ciations of the governor.

"Why should he not meet the reward of
his deeds?" exclaimed their leader, Kidby,
angrily.

"Mayhap it may come yet, but in another
way than he thinketh," said Kirkby.

"What meanest thou, Kirkby?" asked Sinnott.

"The Lord himself judgeth," answered the
other, solemnly.

The magistrates, too, whispering among themselves, found no excuse for their chief, who had so openly and flagrantly set the law at naught. Never kindly in their feelings toward Bellingham, their antagonism was now all the more increased, and an opportunity only was awaited for them openly to show their hostility to him.

Among all the people, none were more outspoken in their disapproval, both of Bellingham and of his wife, than were the women. Sharptongued were some of these Puritan dames, and intolerant of those who were breakers of the law, human or divine. With their consciences braced upon their interpretation of the Scriptures, they could scarcely imagine any punishment too severe for this aristocratic pair of law-breakers. It is not at all certain that, had these women had their will, they would not have condemned the governor and his young wife to an hour in the pillory, or even to a taste of the constable's whip.

ONCE again came the day of the General Court of Elections, and once more the freemen of the colony crowded the streets of Boston. Very like it was to the throng which filled the streets a year ago, but quite unlike was the conversation in the market-stead and at the street corners. Not a voice was heard in praise of Richard Bellingham, nor in urging his re-election. Again and again was told the story of his infraction of the law, of his perfidy toward his friend, and of his defiance of the court. The story was new to none. All had heard it; and what the governor had hoped would increase his popularity was itself the very thing which called forth their execration. It was, then, with exceeding chagrin that Governor Bellingham heard the announcement of Increase Nowell that John Winthrop had been returned to the governor's seat by a great majority of the votes of the freemen. It was a result that he must have anticipated ; yet his chagrin was none the less keen, and was increased by the recollection of his own meagre majority a year before. It was with the bitterness of death that he administered the oath to his successor and surrendered to him his chair of office. That his own deputy-governor, Endicott, was re·elected did not in the least assuage his chagrin. As he withdrew, after the throng of freemen had disappeared and left the General Court to its deliberations, he felt that he was followed by all with a smile of derision. As he emerged into the market-place and faced the throng assembled there, and as they respectfully made way for him, he felt that all eyes were upon him ; and that few, if any, sympathized with him in his disappointment.

"Penelope," he said, as he seated himself
in his library, and drew his young wife toward
him, "the blow hath come upon me. Know
that I am no more Governor Bellingham, and
thou no more the governor's wife. I did fear
as much," he went on, scarcely noticing the
effect of his communication upon his wife,
"when the freemen of Boston did refuse to
return Master Hibbens, who is the husband of
my sister Ann, as a deputy to the General
Court, but elected Captain Gibbons in his
stead.[28]   Even then I feared me that my
magistracy was ended."

"Nay, but the people of Boston did again
elect thee to order the town's affairs, but in
the month after our marriage."[29]

"True, and so they did; but such hath
been the custom, that the governor should
be one of those who order the town's occasions. Now they have scorned me. Winthrop
hath an ambition to be the governor, and
some say that he doth desire that he be

chosen for life. He hath but achieved his opportunity."

" Is Master Winthrop, then, the governor? "

" Even he."

Penelope turned slowly away, and walking to the alcoved window, cast herself in silence upon the crimson cushion. Bellingham regarded her attentively for a time ; but she made no sign. At length he approached and seated himself beside her.

" Penelope, have I wronged thee? I did ask thee to be the governor's wife, and I did offer what was not mine to give," he said.

Penelope made no answer.

"Ah, how blind was I ! " sighed Bellingham. " I did tempt thee with a bubble, which hath broken at a breath. Thou didst violence to thine own heart, and now hast naught to repay thee."

"Nay, nay, say not so ! " said Penelope, starting up. " I still have thee, and thou art all the world. Let all else be forgotten.

Thou art not the governor, but thou art still
Bellingham, and I am thy wife. True will I
be to thee, though thou art in sorrow. Thy
grief is mine also, — not for my own sake, but
for thine. Let the people do as they may.
Some day again thou shalt come into thine
own; and then shall I be the governor's wife,
and thou wilt have kept thy promise."

Bellingham's face lighted with a smile.

"If thou hast no regrets now, thou shalt
have none hereafter."

"Of that I am sure," she answered.

Penelope's words were prophetic; but long
years must pass before their fulfilment, and
both joy and sorrow were to come to her heart
and home. Although deprived of the governorship, the social position which Bellingham
occupied was well assured by his wealth and
education. He was born to be a leader of
men; and although never enjoying an extreme
popularity, he was still much sought for advice
and counsel both in public and in private affairs.

As a selectman of .the town, he was vigilant
and watchful of the public weal. There were
few among the colonists who were possessed of
wealth ; and, following the monarchical system
under which they were born and reared, they
drew a sharp line between the gentry and the
common people. Bred as a lawyer, and possessed of wealth which, for those early days,
was by no means inconsiderable, Bellingham
could not fail to occupy a social position far
above the greater portion of the people about
him. Unlike Winthrop, he failed to draw
the hearts of the people to him ; and he had
not the rugged, bold conscientiousness of Endicott. Excessively opinionated, after the First
Church and the Second Church were gathered,
he could see no good reason for the formation
of a third. Acting upon this belief, he became
the implacable, unyielding enemy of the Third,
or, as it came to be called, the Old South
Church. When the church was finally gathered,
and an edifice had been erected upon what had

been the lawn of Governor Winthrop's mansion, he conceived for the church an opposition
amounting almost to hatred, which ended only
with his life.   Some there were, at the last, who
were fain to rejoice at his death that a "Son of
Belial" had been removed from among them.[30]
But this is anticipating.

However great might be the unpopularity of
her husband, Penelope was, or appeared to be,
blissfully unconscious of it all.   She looked up
to her husband, since he was many years her
senior, much as a child looks to a father for
counsel.   She believed in him, and she thor-
oughly believed that some day he would again
fill the governor's chair.   Although she rapidly
lost her youthful manner, and assumed the airs
of a matron, as became one in her social station, she did not forget her former associates
and friends.   Possessed of a nature far more
genial and sunny than that of her husband, she
made many friends, and lost none.   True, after
her marriage, she was looked upon with cold-

ness by many on account of her conduct toward Ezekiel; but this frost soon dissolved beneath the warmth of her smile, and those friends who had momentarily deserted her returned to their allegiance; nor did she appear to have noticed, and if she did she readily forgave, their resentment toward her. The old mansion on Cotton Hill was filled with warmth and sunshine and the sound of young, fresh voices.

Madame Bellingham was by no means plebeian in her tastes, yet she was not exclusive. Many a worthy young man and maiden who had not been accustomed to mingle in the higher society of the Colony were admitted and welcomed to her charmed circle. Thus did her influence among the people serve to level the social barriers and obliterate distinctions. In fact, the gentry as a class began rapidly to disappear, or rather to become absorbed, despite their struggles, into the great middle class,

Her leadership in the social life of the
Colony was one of the joys that came into the
life of Penelope Bellingham; but there were
others. One by one little ones, charming buds
of promise, came to her home; but these joys
were soon followed by deepest grief. The cup
of happiness was scarcely placed at her lips
ere it was dashed away, and the sweet draught
spilled upon the earth. So came little Hannah
and tiny James, Sarai and Ann and Grace; but
scarcely had the drops of the baptismal waters
touched their foreheads ere they faded away,
and " Rachel, weeping for her children, would
not be comforted because they were not." [81]

Two only of the little band were left to
her: John, a sturdy little lad, and his sister
Elizabeth, a tiny girl, with hair as her
mother's was, of the hue of the morning sunlight. One bright morning in spring-time,
the little one slipped from her nurse's care,
and opening the gate, danced merrily down
the street. Away, away, she knew not, cared

not whither, — only to be free and to hear the
birds sing in the trees, or to play marbles
with the children of the street, whom she had
so often seen and envied from the windows
of her father's house. At last she reached
the landing-place, and stood, bedraggled and
dusty, gazing far out upon the blue waters of
the harbor. Her torn frock fluttered in the
wind, and she swung her hood in her hand
and laughed shrilly as her hair blew in dis-
order about her face. She watched a gray-
haired man, as he rowed slowly toward the
landing-place, made fast his boat, and clam-
bered upon the pier. He had a kindly
eye, and none had ever spoken rudely to
the child. She felt no fear, then, as he
approached and addressed her.

"Who art thou, little one? Hast thou not
wandered from thy home? What is thy
name? Canst tell me?"

"My name?" answered the child. "Oh,
yes! I can tell my name. It is Elizabeth."

"And what is thy other name, little one?"

"I have no other name. I am only Elizabeth."

"But who is thy father?"

"Dost thou not know my father? Thou canst not live in Boston that thou dost not know Master Richard Bellingham. My mother saith that he was once the governor, and that he will be, mayhap, again; but that was long, long, ago, — before ever I was born."

"Thou art Richard Bellingham's child? I knew him once," added the man, as if to himself. "And I knew thy mother, also," he continued, addressing the child, after a pause. "Thou hast thy mother's look in thy face. That, too, was long, long ago; but I have not forgotten," he added, dreamily. He took the child's hand tenderly within his own, and pressed it in his broad palms. Then he softly stroked her hair, and smiled down upon her and said : —

"Thou art far from home for a little one

like thee. Dost thou know the way? Let me lead thee home."

Gently he led the little child along, lifting her tenderly over the rough places, and listening delightedly to her childish prattle by the way. At length they came within sight of the mansion of Bellingham, and the child sprang forward with a cry of delight.

"See! there is my father's house."

"Yea, child, I know it," said the man. "Stay but a moment;" and he loosened a spray of fresh mayflowers from his doublet. "Give thou these to thy mother, child; and say to her that she must care for these blossoms, lest they wither, like the others."

"Yea, I will tell her what thou sayest," said the child; and she tripped away to her home. A moment later she was pouring her tale of her wonderful adventures into her mother's startled ears.

"As I stood upon the pier," said the child. "a good, old man with gray locks and sad eyes, that once looked misty as he talked, came to me and asked me my name. And when I told him, he said that I had wandered from home, and that he knew my father and my mother once, long, long ago, and that he would take me home. He took me by the hand and led me, and he lifted me over the stones, that I fell not; and he brought me to the corner yonder, until I could see my father's house. And he gave to me these flowers," she added, "and he bade me give them to thee, and to say to thee : 'Take care of these flowers, lest they wither like the others.'"

"What was he like, this man, my child?" asked the mother. "Had he deep, blue eyes?"

"Yea, mother, they were deep and dark : but they looked at me so sadly, and when I turned away and looked again he was still looking at me with his sad eyes. Who was he. mother? Dost thou know him?"

"Nay, nay, my child; I know him not. He had gray locks, thou sayest?" As she spoke she gasped slightly, and turned away to hide a tear, and left the room. Once safely in her own chamber, she covered her face with her hands and wailed in anguish.

"My children, my children! He said, 'Alas, the withered blossoms! the withered blossoms!' Can he have had a presage? And he warned me that I tempt not the name of the Lord. Alas, alas! hath the Lord come in judgment upon me? Hath he sent children to me but to mock me? I did call his will what was but my own desire for wealth and power. Oh! that my repentance might save to me these two!" And she wept bitterly.

Alas, woe came again upon her, and as she clasped her little one to her bosom, she faded and was not, and John alone was left as his mother's comforter.

Chapter XIV.

IT has been said that Penelope's words were prophetic, when she assured her husband that some day he would again be the governor of the Colony of Massachusetts Bay. Doubtless, Bellingham little thought that twelve years must pass before he would again be elevated to power. Yet so it was, and even at the expiration of that long period of penance, he was not elevated to the highest place, but was forced to be content to be the deputy-governor only. A year later, he was again given a short lease of the highest office, and once more the people bowed their heads to Governor Bellingham, as he passed; but Penelope, his wife, was no longer the bright young girl who had become the governor's bride. She was now a woman of middle age, among whose golden locks sorrow and care had already drawn, here and there, a line of silver. The governor himself now trod more heavily than of yore, and his locks were gray; but in no wise had he endeared himself to the people more than before. His manner was austere; but this was the manner of the times. It was something more than austerity that was the controlling characteristic of Governor Bellingham's nature. Yet as time passed, the remembrance of many of the failings of his earlier years faded from the minds of the people. Many of his generation, of his early antagonists, passed away, or ceased to be active in the local political arena. The remembrance of his violation of the law and of his lack of personal good faith, in the affair of his marriage, ceased to be discussed, and at last became only a tradition, to be told by the old men and crooning dames, as they warmed their withered hands over the blaze upon the hearth.

Still Bellingham was, for the second time, retained but for a single year in his exalted position. The following year he was again deposed, and Endicott was once more chosen governor. Bellingham's grasp at political power was strong, however, and though, while Endicott lived, he could not attain his highest wishes, still none could wrest from him the second office in the colony. As Deputy-Governor Bellingham, then, we are to know him for ten years to come.

The years which had elapsed between the first and the last election of Bellingham, as governor of the Colony, had been the most eventful which England had ever seen. Only now and then, however, when a ship arrived, bringing supplies and welcome additions to their number, did the colonists learn of the great events that were happening across the sea. Then they heard of the great contest which was waged between Parliament and the throne. They heard that their countrymen had taken up arms against one another, and that great battles were fought between those whom they deemed to be their friends and the troops led by the king. They heard that the Puritan Cromwell had arisen almost from obscurity, and had become the great leader of the cause of the people. They heard, at last, and they told it with bated breath and in startled whispers, in the market-place and about the streets, that Charles had laid his royal head upon the block, and that king-craft, in England, with him had died. They heard and rejoiced that, upon the ruins of the monarchy, had arisen a commonwealth, which they regarded as the realization of their dreams of religious freedom and the extinction of popery.

Their exultation was not of long duration. One day a ship arrived bringing the dread news that Cromwell was dead, and that the second Charles, already the crowned King of Scotland, had been restored to the English throne. The adherents of Cromwell were flying for their lives, or were laying their heads upon the block. The same ship brought three mysterious strangers, who shrank from the gaze of men, and soon disappeared from the settlement as mysteriously as they came. Who were these men, was a question that long puzzled the gossips of the town. Endicott and Bellingham and others of the magistrates knew that these were of that bold band of men who had sat in judgment upon their king and had condemned him to death.

It was not alone in England that tragedies were enacted. From the superstition of the time sprang the delusion which, a few years later, in Salem, wrought such atrocities as make men shudder even now, when they are recalled. Upon the family of Bellingham was the blow the first to fall.

The deputy-governor, despairing and helpless to save her from her dreadful fate, saw
his sister led forth to death.[32] Thus another
and a blacker shadow fell upon Richard
Bellingham's life.

With the death of Endicott was removed
the last obstacle to the full realization of
Bellingham's hopes. Twice had he been
elected governor, but for only a year at each
time had he enjoyed his exaltation. There
were those who, following the superstitious
ideas of the day, fully believed that to his
faithlessness to Ezekiel might be ascribed all
his woes and disappointments. Some said
that the young secretary's gesture, at parting
with the governor and Penelope, upon their
bridal evening, was an unuttered curse; and
that this, hovering like a cloud above the two,
hung between them and the sunlight of happiness. As one by one the little ones were
laid away in the tomb, the more superstitious
among the townspeople shook their heads

gravely and whispered one to another, as the funerals passed : " Behold ! here is yet another withered blossom." When, for the second time, Bellingham failed to hold the lofty position that he had acquired, a few were left of these, who said solemnly among themselves : " Nay, but this must needs be so. Bellingham hath brought upon himself his own debasement."

At length his last rival for gubernatorial honors was gone. Winthrop had preceded Endicott to the unseen country by nearly a score of years. Dudley, too, was gone, and now, save Bellingham, scarce one remained of that band of leaders who for so many years had stood at the head of the affairs of state. He was an old man now. Twenty-four years had passed since first he claimed the title of governor. Now, at last, when he had come into the full fruition of a life-long hope,[33] his youth and middle age were long past. A childless old man, too, he was; for John, the hope of his years, a young man, stalwart and strong, the son of his old age, had been taken.[34]

This last was a crushing blow to Governor Bellingham and to his wife, Penelope. As they stood by the open tomb, where already they had laid away so much of precious dust, the stern old man stood immovable amid the throng of onlookers, and gave no token of the great grief with which his proud heart was filled; but Penelope, as she gazed down into the gulf, and saw at her feet the row of tiny coffins, remembered suddenly her dream of years before. As vividly as then she saw the row of graves, now become to her a terrible reality; and as she turned away from the tomb and left, in his long sleep, the last child of her heart, her tearful eyes met a look of the deepest sympathy and sorrow upon an unfamiliar face.

Then, again, came to her mind her dream, and she saw once more, but now in the flesh, the sad, patient face, fringed about with hair like hoar-frost. 'She saw the deep, blue eyes, and in them that same look of unutterable love, which was cast upon her when Ezekiel, her betrothed and forsaken, left her presence forever. She went to her home and wept.

Governor Bellingham, when alone in his chamber, paced the floor with clenched hands, and cried aloud in his agony: " Oh, my son, Absalom ! my son, my son Absalom ! Would God I had died for thee, O Absalom ! my son, my son ! "

Governor Bellingham did not long survive his son. Beyond his threescore years and ten when last chosen governor, he was readily persuaded to allow the younger and more vigorous deputy-governor, Willoughby, and later the ambitious Leverett, to perform many of the functions of the higher office. When the son of his old age was taken from him, his heart broke. For two years he lingered,

until he had fully rounded his fourscore years ;
but one day, when the leaves were yellow
upon the trees, a long procession wound its
way to the old burying-ground, and Richard
Bellingham was gathered to his fathers.[35]

The stern old man's career was ended, and
beside the son whom he so greatly loved, and
the little children who had come to him only
for a season, he was laid away to rest.   A
great concourse looked on in solemn silence.
Among them all there was but one soul which
grieved for him, — one whose once golden locks
were now turned to silver, though more from
grief than age ; for she had sold a heart's love
for wealth and station, and had purchased but
an empty token.   What now remained to
Penelope, save a generation of widowhood, a
faded ribbon close about her neck, and a
hope of immortality?

But what of Governor Bellingham?   A
Nemesis had followed him through life, and

even in the grave, where all troubles of this
earth should end, it still pursued him. Suns
rose and set; seasons came and went; the
Province succeeded the Colony; a war for
liberty came, and the waves of conflict surged
about his resting-place. Soldiers clad in scarlet
played cards upon his tombstone. Then the
forces of Britain were driven back, and peace
came and spread her white wings over a long-
stricken people. Then came a long line of
governors of a free state, and one of these
sought a place of sepulture for his family. The
old burying-ground was crowded with silent
forms, mustered thither through a century and
a half of living and dying. Then said Governor Sullivan : " Behold here is the tomb of
this ancient governor of the Colony. Who,
indeed, was Richard Bellingham, save, as the
records tell us, for a while, a hundred years
ago, governor of the Colony of Massachusetts
Bay? He has no descendants to claim or to

care for his resting-place. Why should not
I, James Sullivan, claim this tomb to be
mine?"

It was so ordered by the selectmen of the
town, and the name of another was carved
above that of Richard Bellingham, upon his
tombstone.[36] It came to pass, in the lapse of
time, that Governor Sullivan, too, was gathered to his fathers, and once more was seen
a great concourse of people following a governor's bier to his resting-place. It is many
years ago that Governor Sullivan was laid away
for his long sleep beside Governor Bellingham. Still, it is one of the traditions which
hover about the old Granary Burying-ground
in Boston, that they who opened the tomb,
whose entrance had been sealed for a hundred years, started, with a sudden horror, at
that which was revealed. Lo! the earth
itself, from which we all sprang, and to
which we must return, had recoiled from him

who would betray a friend. Gushing from its depths, a spring had bubbled forth and filled the space; and upon the surface of the dark water floated an ancient oaken coffin. Upon its lid was written the name of Richard Bellingham.[87]

Chapter XV.

LITTLE remains to be recorded. Penelope Bellingham, a sad-faced widow, went from her husband's grave to her deserted mansion. It was but a step or two distant, and from certain windows of her home she might see, if she would, the tomb which held all for which she had lived. It is said that from these windows the lonely woman never looked, and passers-by remarked that at them the curtains were never drawn. Trouble and sorrow, to which she had been no stranger for years, did not desert her now. The records of the courts of Massachusetts contain no such long-contested suit

14

at law as that which, for one hundred and
fourteen years, was waged concerning the
last will and testament of Governor Bellingham.   During the thirty long years of her
widowhood she knew no day when the wealth
for which she bargained the love of her
youth was not the subject of legal controversy.   At Chelsea, at Ipswich, at Salem, she
tarried for a time, as if to seek rest for a
troubled spirit; but as surely as the metal
returns to the lodestone, so did Madame
Bellingham return to the place of her triumph and of her sorrow.   She seldom looked
upon the tomb which held her all; for insep-
arable from it was the mental vision of those
sad eyes which looked upon her once and
yet again, so full of love and of compassion.
On rare occasions was she seen in public.
Sometimes, at dusk, attended only by a servant, would she venture forth from her gloomy
mansion, from whose quaint windows the light
of social hospitality never shone.   The younger

people of the town looked upon her with
reverence, mingled with awe; the children
regarded the mysterious woman with dread,
and fled if they saw her approaching in the
gloaming. At infrequent intervals she attended church, where she sat with other
aged dames or spinsters in the foreseat for
women.[88] As the congregation dispersed, she
would return with silent dignity the greetings
of these relics of a past age, and of the very
few who remained of her husband's contem-
poraries. These formalities over, she would
hasten away, with downcast eyes and closely
drawn veil, as if fearful lest she might encounter one whose glance would bring to her
heaviness of spirit for days to come.

Meanwhile, great matters were happening in
the mother-country across the sea. The second
Charles had flashed and revelled and died, a
disappointed man that he had left none of his
line to succeed him; the second James had
mounted the throne only to view from its height

a sea of blood, and at last, a fugitive, he was
king no longer; and the first of the line
of Protestant monarchs ascended England's
throne. William and Mary reigned together
over Britain; then Mary died, and William
was left to rule alone.

One bright day in May, 1702, a great buzz-
ing was heard in the market-place and about
the streets of Boston. A town house had been
built in the open stead since the days of Governor Bellingham, where all the public affairs
were transacted. About this were clustered
groups of excited men. Not a few women,
too, attracted by the unusual concourse, paused
to learn the meaning of it all. There were not
many in the throng whom we saw gathered
here upon the morning of Bellingham's first
election. More than sixty years had passed
since that memorable morning. Here and
there was seen an aged man, whose thin, white
locks told of a generation long past. There
were others, gray-haired men too, who in

recalling their childhood's days told of that bright June morning, when Winthrop and Endicott and Bellingham and Saltonstall walked together in the solemn procession.

" How now?" asked a late comer. " What meaneth this great concourse? Hast news of moment from our lord the king?"

" News, indeed!" answered the man addressed. " But an hour agone arrived at the town house Master Burrington, who cometh from Newfoundland. He bringeth to the magistrates prints which tell of the death of our most valiant king."

"God rest his soul!"

" Amen!" responded the other. " And the magistrates are but now met together within the town house, and the speech of all is that, soon after midday, a proclamation shall be made to the people, that the virtuous Princess Anne hath become our queen."

" Long live her Gracious Majesty!"

So ran the gossip of the town; and rapidly

the tidings flew, from street to street, from house to house, until all had heard the great news. Then were seen, hurrying to the place of rendezvous, soldiers bearing their glittering halberds. Now and then, amid the din, was heard the sound of a drum or fife. At length amid the excited throng in the market-place went up a shrill cry, —

"Back, good people, back ! They come ! "

A sudden hush followed. Then the people, parting upon either side, made way for the grand procession. Crowded in a vast throng, they stood in solemn silence. Upon paling and gate-post were clustered the boys and the youth of the town. Even the roofs were black with human forms; while the windows which afforded a view of the market-stead were filled with the matrons and maidens, interested spectators of the scene below. No sound but the tramp of the coming procession broke the stillness.

First came into view a platoon of horsemen,

their brilliant uniforms and polished halberds glittering in the sun. Behind them came the company of artillery, though Robert Keayne no longer marched at its head. Then came the civic procession, — the representatives to the General Court, the ministers, the justices in their robes of office, and citizens of wealth and prominence. Last of all came the life-guard of horse, escorting the Council of State, which that year performed the gubernatorial functions. Halting at the head of the market-place, the regiment divided into two ranks, which, facing inward, were aligned upon either side of the open stead. Before the town house, in the centre of the open space, stood the color-bearer, holding aloft the standard of Britain. Within the lines of soldiery on either side were ranged the dignitaries, civil and ecclesiastical, who had formed a part of the solemn procession.

When all were in their places, Sheriff Gookin advanced to the centre of the open stead, and

in a loud voice, though surely it seemed quite
unnecessary, commanded all to keep silence.
Then a figure, clad in black velvet, left his
place among the ranks of official personages,
and took his position beneath the folds
of England's flag. It was Mr. Secretary
Addington.

A deeper silence than before fell upon the
vast assemblage. All listened for his voice;
and soon, clear and full, it broke upon the air.
In breathless silence the great throng stood
until the last words of the proclamation of
Anne as Queen of England had died away.
Then, amid the rolling of drums, long and
loud burst forth from every throat a great
cry, —

"Long live the Queen!"

Slowly the great crowd dispersed, and as
they went the church bells took up the joyful
refrain. From out their brazen throats rang
forth a pæan of solemn rejoicing, sending far
out over the sea, as if striving to reach the

farther shore, the joyful tones of welcome to the sovereign of England, Old and New.

Suddenly the tones of rejoicing ceased, and, as the last tremulous vibrations thrilled the air and died away in space, a hush pervaded the town. All stilled their sounds of merry-making, and looking at each other, said, —

"Behold, what meaneth this sudden silence?"

In a moment more the bell began a solemn toll; and then all knew that amid the rejoicing some soul had passed to its final account. A breathless, awe-struck stillness fell upon all as at last the tolling ceased. Then after a pause, while all wondered who it was that had passed, the bell, in measured but rapid strokes, again began its utterance.

"One, two, three, four, five, six, seven, eight, nine, ten — "

"It cannot be a child, then, whose soul has passed," said the listeners.

" Fifteen, sixteen, seventeen, eighteen — "

" It can be no youth," said another.

" Nor yet a young man or woman," argued a third, as the strokes reached and passed the twenties and entered upon the thirties.

Still the bell tolled on.   Forty, fifty, and sixty were passed; and then the feeling of solemn awe deepened upon the listening town.

" Who, forsooth, can it be whose spirit hath passed?" said they, one to another.   "Surely it must be one of the fathers or mothers in Israel."

The bell strokes numbered eighty, and all the town was breathless.   Then, after a slight pause, the tones rang out two strokes more. Then there was a great silence.

" It is Madame Bellingham who is gone from us," said one of a group which clustered before the meeting-house.   "There is none other among us who is of the age of eighty-two."

The speaker was a sad-faced old man, whose deep blue eyes filled with tears as he spoke. There was none other to shed a tear; but solemnly and reverently all bared their heads, and said in unison, —

"God rest her soul!"

Again a long procession of the people of the town followed a bier to the ancient burying-place. There were few amid all the great throng who had ever looked upon the face of her who had gone, or had heard the sound of her voice; and when the stone which covered the tomb was at last sealed for a hundred years of undisturbed repose, the crowd melted away, and soon was gone. A few, who still lingered in the gloaming, and spoke in whispers of the aged woman whose life had ended, saw an old man slowly and softly approach the tomb, and lay something upon it. Then he as softly stole away again, and was lost in the dusk.

Then some, more bold and curious than the rest, drew near to learn what the old man's mysterious offering might be ; and they, who had never heard the story of Ezekiel and Penelope, marvelled that it was only a cluster of fresh mayflowers, bound about with a faded ribbon.

APPENDIX.

1. PAGE 13. — The psalms on pages 12, 13, and 15 are from the "Bay Psalm Book," Cambridge, 1639, — doubtless the first book published in America.

2. PAGE 28. — Rev. John Wilson, minister of the First Church in Boston.

3. PAGE 29. — Vide "Boston Town Records," vol. i., "Reports of Record Commissioners": "This 28th of 12th moneth, 1641, It's Ordered that the Constables shall pay unto Arthur Perry 4*l.*, 10*s.* for his service in drumming the last yeare, Ending this present day."

4. PAGE 30. — Vide "New England Historic-Genealogical Register," 1850, p. 299. "Penelope Pelham, sister of Herbert Pelham, came over on the Susan and Ellen in 1635. . . . She was then 16 years old." Sir Richard Saltonstall and his wife are recorded as coming in the same ship.

5. PAGE 33. — In the year 1640 Thomas Dudley was governor of the Colony of Massachusetts Bay, and Richard Bellingham deputy-governor.

6. PAGE 35. — Vide "Boston Town Records,"
1640, p. 41; "Second Report of Boston Record
Commissioners," p. 51 : "The 30th day of the 1st
moneth, March, 1640. At a Meeting this day of
Mr John Winthrop, Governor, Captaine Edward
Gibon, Mr William Colbrow, Mr William Ting,
Mr John Cogan and Jacob Elyott.   .   .   .   .

Also it is agreed that William Hudson, the
Elder, shalbe Commended to the Court, that he
may have Allowance to Keepe an Ordinary."

7. PAGE 35. — Ibid., p. 5 : "The 8th day
of the 6th moneth, 1635. Nicholys Willys was
Chosen a Constable for this following yeare and
hath taken his oath accordingly." Ibid., p. 87 :
"23, 1 mo., 46, Nicholas Willis, James Everill,
Tho. Grubb, Robt. Tourner, Shoomaker, Constables, for this yeare."

8. PAGE 35. — Ibid., p. 7 : "The 23d of the
11th moneth, 1635. Att a general meeting upon
publique notice. Imprymis at this meeting, Thomas Marshall is, by generall consent, chosen for
the Keeping of a ferry from the mylne point into
Charlestowne on to Wynnyseemitt and to take for
his ferrying into Charlestowne, as the ferry man
there hath, and unto Wynnyseemitt for a single
person, 6*d*.; for two, 6*d*.; and for every one above
the number of two, 2*d*. a peece."

9. PAGE 38. — Herbert Pelham was treasurer of Harvard College in 1643, — a slight anachronism.

10. PAGE 39. — Bellingham and his wife Eliza — or, as one authority says, Elizabeth — became members of the First Church, Boston, in 1634. There is no record of her death upon the town records, but it must have occurred between that date and 1641, the date of his second marriage.

11. PAGE 39. — The author has taken some liberties with the exact chronological order of events. The date of Samuel Bellingham's return to England cannot be fixed, but it must have been subsequent to 1645, since a deed of Edward Bendell, witnessed by Samuel Bellingham, and bearing that date, is recorded in " The Book of Possessions," p. 43.

12. PAGE 41. — " The Book of Possessions," p. 5, records this as " One house and Lott, about a quarter of an acre, bounded on the east with the street; Christopher Stanley, John Biggs, James Browne and Alexander Becke on the south; Joshua Scott on the west; and Mr. William Tynge on the north." The lot upon Cotton Hill, upon which Governor Bellingham built his mansion, is described in " The Book of Possessions,"

as "a garden plott, bounded with Mr. John Cotton and Daniell Maude on the north; the highway uppon the east; John Coggan on the south."

13. PAGE 42. — Cf. "The Scarlet Letter," chap. vii.

14. PAGE 44. — The Ancient and Honorable Artillery Company of Boston was founded by Robert Keayne, who was its first commander, in 1638. The Company has had a continuous existence to the present time.

15. PAGE 54. — Vide "Second Report of Boston Record Commissioners," p. 160, "Boston Town Records," vol. i. p. 165: "12th of the 6th, August, 1636. At a general meeting of the richer inhabitants there was given toward the maintenance of a free school master for the youth with us, Mr Daniel Maud being now also chosen thereunto : —

The Governor, Mr Henry Vane, Esq x *l.*
The Deputy Governor, Mr. John Winthrop, Esq. x *l.*
Mr. Richard Bellingham, xl *s.*" — etc.

It will be seen that the author has taken some liberty with the chronological order of events, committing a slight anachronism. The date of the above record is 1636; the author places it at 1640. Vane returned to England in 1637, and was knighted in 1640.

16. PAGE 60.—That such was the custom of warning inhabitants of public meetings is shown in vol. i. "Boston Town Records," p. 57: "This 10th of the 11th moneth, 1641. At a generall Townsmeeting, upon warning from house to house—"

17. PAGE 65.—In later years the famous Bunch of Grapes Tavern. This was occupied as a public house from 1640, when William Hudson was granted "an allowance to Keepe an Ordinary," to 1760, when this and neighboring buildings were destroyed by fire. Cf. "Second Report of Boston Record Commissioners," part 2 (City Document 46), p. 99.

18. PAGE 71.—Vide "Second Report of Boston Record Commissioners," part 1, p. 52: "The 20th day of the 2d moneth, called Aprill, 1640. Att a Generall meeting upon publique notice. At this meeting Captaine Edward Gibon and Mr. Willyam Tinge Chosen for the Comittees or Deputyes of this Towne for this next General Court." Ibid., p. 61: "This 27th of the 3d moneth, 1641. Att a generall Towne meeting, upon publique notice, Mr. William Tynge, Treasurer, and Mr. William Hibbens are chosen Deputyes for the service of the generall Court."

19. PAGE 81.—Vide "John Winthrop's History

of New England," vol. ii p. 42 : "Some of the freemen without the consent of the magistrates had chosen Mr. Nathaniel Ward to preach at this court, pretending that it was a part of their liberty. The governor (whose right indeed it is, for, till the court be assembled the freemen are but private persons) would not strive about it, for though it did not belong to them, yet if they would have it, there was reason to yield to them. Yet they had no great reason to choose him, though otherwise very able, seeing he had cast off his pastor's place at Ipswich, and was now no minister by the received determination of our churches. In his sermon he delivered many useful things, but in a moral and political discourse, grounding his propositions much upon the old Roman and Grecian governments, which sure is an error, for if religion and the Word of God make men wiser than their neighbors, and these times have the advantage of all that have gone before us in experience and observation, it is probable that, by all these helps we may better frame rules of government for ourselves than to receive others upon the bare authority of the wisdom, justice, &c., of these heathen commonwealths. Among other things he advised the people to keep all their magistrates in an equal rank and not

give more honor or power to one than to another.
Another advice he gave, that magistrates should
not give private advice and take knowledge of
any man's cause before it came to public hear-
ing. This was debated after in the general
court, when some of the deputies moved to have
it ordered."

20. PAGE 84. — Vide "John Winthrop's History
of New England," vol. ii. p. 41: "I must here
return to supply what was omitted concerning
the proceedings of the last court of elections.
There had been much laboring to have Mr. Bellingham chosen, and when the votes were numbered he had six more than the others; but there
were divers who had not given in their votes,
who now came into the court and desired their
liberty, which was denied by some of the magistrates, because they had not given them in at
the doors. But others thought it was an injury,
yet were silent, because it concerned themselves,
for the order of giving in their votes at the door
was no order of court, but only direction of some
of the magistrates; and without question, if any
freeman tender his vote before the election be
passed and published it ought to be received."

21. PAGE 86. — Vide "Records of the Colony
of Massachusetts Bay in New England," June 2,

1641. "The order formerly made for allowing 100*l.* p. @ to the Govr is repealed."

22. PAGE 96. — "1639, 7 mo 9. For preventing of all unlawful mariages, &c., it is ordered that, after duoe publication of this order, noe persons shalbee joined in marriage before the intention of the parties proceeding therein hath bene three times· published at some time of publick lecture or towne meeting, in both the townes where the parties, or either of them do ordinarily reside; and in such townes where no lectures are, then the same intention to be set up in writing, upon some poast standing in public view and used for such purposes onely and there to stand, so as it may easily bee read by the space of fourteen days." — *Records of the Colony of Massachusetts Bay in New England,* 1639.

23. PAGE 102. — King's Chapel Burying-ground, so called; the first burial-ground of the colony, established in one corner of "Isaac Johnson's field," which comprised the great square, bounded by the streets now known as Tremont, School, Washington, and Court streets. In Andros's time a portion of this burial-ground was taken for the use of the Church of England, and a church erected thereon. This church and its successor were, and are now, known as King's Chapel, and

the burial-ground subsequently became known by the same name.

24. PAGE 149. — Vide " Suffolk County (Mass.) Land Records," lib. viii. fol. 298: A deed, by affidavit of three persons, from Governor Richard Bellingham, deceased, to Angola, a negro, in reward for saving the life of the governor, "comeing to me with his boat, when I was sunke in the river, betwene Boston and Winisimet, severall years since, & layd hold of mee & got me into the boat, he came in and saved my life, which Kindnese of him I remember; and besides my giveing him fifty foot square of my land, to him & his, I shall see hee shall not want whilst I live." This unique deed is published in Vol. V. of " Reports of Boston Record Commissioners," p. 23.

25. PAGE 153. — Ibid. : " John Clough, Junior, aged forty-seven or thereabouts, deposed, saith that hee was present neere the place above mentioned in James Penniman's deposition, & at that tyme, and saw the late Governor Richard Bellingham, Esqr. on his bay horse, sitting."

26. PAGE 160. — Vide " John Winthrop's History of New England," 1641, mo. 9. 9. : " The governor, Mr. Bellingham was married. (I would not mention such ordinary matters in our history

but by occasion of some remarkable accidents.)
The young gentlewoman was ready to be contracted to a friend of his, who lodged in his
house, and by his consent had proceeded so far
with her, when on a sudden the governor treated
with her and obtained her for himself. He ex-
cused it by the strength of his affection and that
she was not absolutely promised to the other
gentleman. Two errors more he committed upon it.
1, That he would not have his contract published
where he dwelt, contrary to an order of court.
2, That he married himself, contrary to the con-
stant practice of the country."

27. PAGE 179. — "John Winthrop's History of
New England," 1641. "The great inquest presented him for breach of the order of court,
and at the court following, in the 4th month, the
secretary called him to answer the prosecution,
but he not going off the bench, as the manner
was, and but few of the magistrates present, he
put it off to another time, intending to speak with
him privately, and with the rest of the magistrates
about the case, and accordingly he told him the
reason why he did not proceed, viz., being unwilling to command him publicly to go off the
bench, and yet not thinking it fit he should sit
as a judge, when he was by law to answer as an

offender. This he took ill, and said he would not go off the bench except he were commanded."

28. PAGE 184.— Vide "Reports of Boston Record Commissioners," vol. ii. p. 65. "This 2d of 3d moneth, 1642. At a general Townsmeeting, upon warning from house to house, William Tyng, Treasurer and Capt. Gibones are chosen Deputyes for the next Generall Court."

29. PAGE 184 — Ibid., p. 65. "This 6th of the 10th moneth, 1641. At a generall Towns meeting, upon Publique warning. There are chosen for the Affayres of the Towne for these six months next ensuing, Richard Bellingham, esqre. Governor, John Winthrop, esqre., William Tynge, Treasurer, Captaine Gibones, Williame Calbron, Jacob Eliott, Valentine Hill, James Penne, John Olivr."

30. PAGE 188.— Vide " Diary of Samuel Sewall," publications of the Massachusetts Historical Society, vol. ii. "The most to be regretted is his enmity to the foundation of the third church of Boston that ceased only with his life." Governor Coddington of Rhode Island is recorded as rejoicing at his death, calling him "Son of Bélial."

31. PAGE 190. — Vide " Reports of Boston Record Commissioners," vol. ix. (City Document 130).

32. PAGE 201. — Mrs. Ann Hibbens, widow of
William Hibbens, and sister of Deputy-Governor
Bellingham, hanged for witchcraft on Boston
Common, June, 1656. Vide "New England Historical and Genealogical Register," vol. vi. p. 283;
also, "Hutchinson Papers," published by the Massachusetts Historical Society, second series, vol. vi.;
also, "Records and Archives of the Massachusetts
General Court," 1656.

33. PAGE 202. — Richard Bellingham was
deputy-governor of the Colony of Massachusetts
Bay in 1635, and again in 1640. In 1641 he was
elected governor, but held that office but one year.
In 1653 he was again elected deputy-governor,
and in 1654 was for a single year advanced to
the position of governor. In 1655 he was made
deputy-governor, and held that office by successive
re-elections, with Endicott as governor, until the
death of the latter in 1665. Bellingham was then
elected governor, and held that office until his
death in 1672, at the age of eighty-one years.

34. PAGE 203. — John Bellingham, son of
Richard and Penelope Bellingham, graduated at
Harvard College in 1660, and died about the
year 1670.

35. PAGE 205. — Governor Richard Bellingham died December 7, 1672, in the eighty-first

year of his age. Vide his tombstone in Granary Burying-ground, Boston.

36. PAGE 207. — Ibid. : " The Bellingham family being extinct, the selectmen of Boston, in the year 1782, assigned this tomb to James Sullivan, Esquire."

37. PAGE 208. — Vide Shurtleff's "Topographical and Historical Description of Boston," p. 214 : " The soil was springy and exceedingly damp. . . . It is said that when Judge Sullivan, at the close of the last century, repaired the Bellingham tomb, he found the coffin and remains of the old governor — who died on the seventh of December, 1672, in the eighty-first year of his age — floating around in the ancient vault."

38. PAGE 211. — Vide " Diary of Samuel Sewall " : " Madame Bellingham in the foreseat for women."

39. PAGE 217. — Vide " Diary of Samuel Sewall," vol. ii. " May 28, 1702. Burrington from Newfoundland brings prints of the King's death, March 8 at 8 A.M. . . . At last the Gazette containing the proclaiming the Queen came to hand. Then we resolved to proclaim her Majesty here, which was done accordingly, below the Townhouse. Regiment drawn up and Life Guards of Horse; Council, Representatives, Ministers,

Justices, Gentlemen taken with the Guard. Mr. Secretary on foot read the order of the Council, the Proclamation and Queen's Proclamation for continuing Commissions. Mr. Sheriff Gookin gave it to the people. Volleys, guns. Proclamation was made between 3 and 4 o'clock. At 5 P.M. Madam Bellingham dies, a vertuous Gentlewoman, *antiquis moribus, prisca fide,* who has lived a widow just about 30 years."

THE END.

Carine, A Story of Sweden.

By LOUIS ÉNAULT. Translated from the French by LINDA DE KOWALEWSKA. With thirty-nine illustrations by LOUIS K. HARLOW. 16mo, *cloth, gilt top*, $1.25.

A New Volume of Poems
BY NORA PERRY.

Lyrics and Legends. By NORA PERRY, author of "After the Ball," "Her Lover's Friend, and Other Poems," "A Flock of Girls and their Friends," "Another Flock of Girls," etc. Illustrated by E. H. GARRETT. 16mo, *cloth, gilt top*, $1.25.

The Blind Musician.

Translated from the Russian of VLADIMIR KOROLENKO by ALINE DELANO. With Introduction by GEORGE KENNAN and illustrations by EDMUND H. GARRETT. 16mo, *cloth, gilt top*, $1.25.

This unique and exquisite little book is less a story than a wonderfully faithful and delicate study in psychology. Though told in prose, it is in essence a poem. — *Boston Transcript.*

It is a marvel of typographical excellence, and the story is worthy of its setting. — *New York Sun.*

A touching and truthful story. — *Boston Gazette.*

www.ingramcontent.com/pod-product-compliance
Lightning Source LLC
Chambersburg PA
CBHW020848270326
41928CB00006B/603